Praise for *The Tree of Sorrow*

Richard D. Bank's richly rewarding memoir spans an era from the early 50's to the Vietnam War. It will speak most strongly to those who experienced Jewish life, in Philadelphia and beyond, during this era. But it does so much more. Bank is a writer's writer. He sees into people, situations, events. His descriptions — of Elie Wiesel and Adolph Eichmann, of Strawberry Mansion and Woodside Park — glow with uncanny detail. His insights are leavened with humility and humor, imbibed throughout with the author's struggles with his own evolving Jewish identity. *The Tree of Sorrow* is indeed more than a memoir. It is a confession, a chronicle, an argument. For justice. For accepting human frailty, admiring human strength. When it ends, the Tree of Sorrow has turned for the writer into a Tree of Hope. I believe him!

  – Harry Ringel, author of *Shemhazai's Game* and *The Phantom of Skid Row*

More Praise for *The Tree of Sorrow*

Filled with rich detail, narrative, and dialogue, *The Tree of Sorrow* fully immerses the reader into an unforgettable journey towards love, loss, and transcendence. Richard D. Bank skillfully describes what it was like to grow up in the shadow of those who lived through the Holocaust. Not only does the reader come to better understand the way the cancer of anti-Semitism changes lives, but also that there is something abiding in the human heart that allows even those who have witnessed unspeakable horrors to continue to love. The author remembers his family and their struggles, and in so doing, pays homage. *The Tree of Sorrow*, along with Richard D. Bank's other books, *I Am Terezin* and *Feig*, are poignant, masterfully crafted, and essential reads for those wanting to learn more about the Holocaust.

– Ayesha F. Hamid, author of the memoir
The Borderland Between Worlds

The Tree of Sorrow
Growing up in the Shadow of the Holocaust

Richard D. Bank

www.auctuspublishers.com

Auctus Publishers

Copyright © 2021 Richard D. Bank

Book and Cover Design by Colleen Cummings

Published by Auctus Publishers

606 Merion Avenue, First Floor

Havertown, PA 19083

Printed in the United States of America

The Tree of Sorrow: Growing Up in the Shadow of the Holocaust is a work of creative non-fiction. The events recounted are to the author's best memory. Some names have been altered to protect the privacy of those involved.

All rights reserved. Scanning, uploading, and distribution of this book via the internet or via any other means without permission in writing from its publisher, Auctus Publishers, is illegal and punishable by law. Please purchase only authorized electronic edition of the book.

ISBN: 978-1-7334456-8-9 (Print)

ISBN: 978-1-7334456-9-6 (Electronic)

Library of Congress Control Number: 2021937589

Dedication

For the Frank and Steinberger Families
To those who perished in the Holocaust
To those who survived
To those who bear the responsibility to remember

In memory of Ludwig and Sophie (nee Steinberger) Frank
Who survived the concentration camp Theresienstadt

In memory of Ruth (nee Frank) Bank
Who became a Holocaust refugee in 1937

The Frank Family Tree

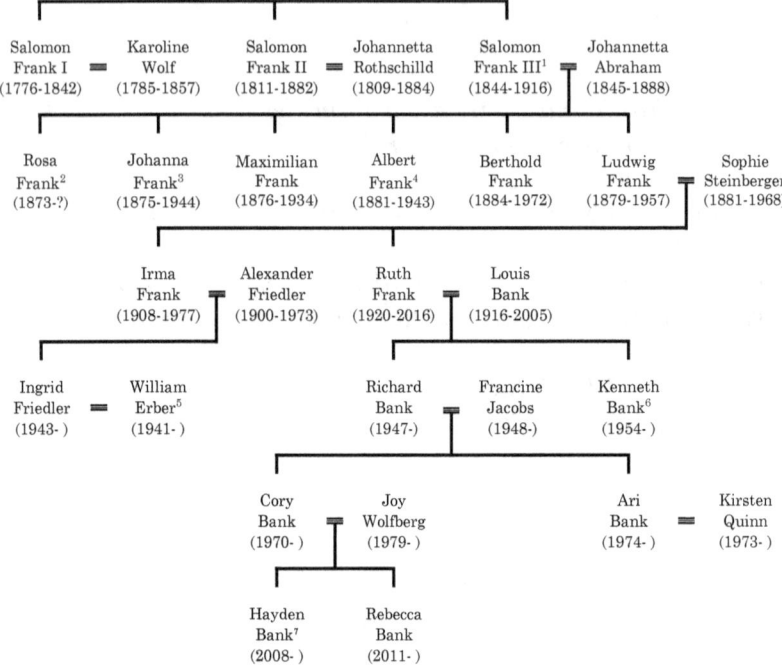

NOTES:

[1] Thus far there are seventy-four descendants of Solomon Frank III and Johannetta who survived or were born after the Holocaust. Each one is a testament that the Nazis failed in their goal to rid the world of Jews.

[2] Rosa Frank along with her husband, Louis Heilbronn, their daughter, Johanna, and granddaughters, Elsbeth, Imgard and Helga, were transported from the Lodz ghetto to Auschwitz where they were murdered.

[3] Johanna Frank died in the concentration camp Theresienstadt.

[4] Albert Frank and his wife Henriette, their son, Heinz, their daughter Irma and her husband Richard Wertheimer, were transported from the Westerbork camp to Auschwitz where they were murdered.

[5] Ingrid and Bill Erber have five children and eleven grandchildren.

[6] Kenneth Bank married Nancy Anderson. They have two children, Edward and Katherine.

[7] The family tree above is part of a larger project undertaken in 2020, by Hayden Bank to create the Frank Family Tree spanning eight generations. At the time of this publication, the work is nearing completion and it is planned that it will be presented at a family reunion.

Introduction

"I just tell stories," the unassuming man said to the group of us seated before him in a nearly empty auditorium that fall evening in 1967, a room which doubled as the sanctuary of a synagogue, one of several serving the Jewish community in Philadelphia's northwest suburbs. These grandiose edifices, situated along a major thoroughfare and looming over neighboring buildings, bore testament that its congregants had successfully made it out of middle-class neighborhoods teeming with rowhouses to affluent communities where most homes nestled on spacious, luxuriant grounds. In fact, one of these houses of worship, Beth Sholom, was designed by the renowned architect Frank Lloyd Wright, and it dominated the panorama with its modernistic, glistening spire boldly rising toward the heavens, something I always thought to be ostentatious and nothing like the synagogues and small shuls I was accustomed to before my family moved to the suburbs in 1960.

That night, I was in one of these synagogues, Adath Jeshurun, which sponsored the evening's program. Up until a few weeks earlier, I had never heard of the speaker

The Tree of Sorrow

and I suppose neither did most of Adath Jeshurun's congregants which likely explained the sparse attendance. In fact, the only reason I was there was because he wrote a book that was required reading in a class I was taking as an undergrad at Temple University. The course was entitled Modern Jewish Thought, and the professor, Maurice Friedman, arguably the world's foremost scholar of Martin Buber, had included the speaker's book in the syllabus along with more prominent theologians such as Abraham Joshua Heschel, Mordecai Kaplan and, of course, Martin Buber. Professor Friedman also said that he knew the speaker personally and thought we would find him of interest if we could make it.

At the time, I was living at home and commuting to Temple, and if it weren't for the fact that Adath Jeshurun was a mere five-minute drive away, it wasn't likely I would have attended. But with little else to do that weekday evening, and savvy enough to want to gain the good graces of my professor, I hastily excused myself from my family's dinner table, hopped in my car and made my way to a practically vacant parking lot at the rear of the synagogue's building. I was surprised to see the sanctuary occupied by no more than twenty people, half a dozen of whom were my fellow students seated on the front row with Professor Friedman whose trademark black beret was prominently visible even from where I entered. I made my way to the front, taking a seat off to the side but on the same row where Professor Friedman sat so he would notice me and hopefully remember that I showed up. Glancing my way, he smiled. Mission accomplished.

I don't remember the introduction, but within a few minutes, the speaker was standing before the group—not up on the podium but just a few feet away from the first row. He was a slight man with a wavy, unruly head of hair atop an angular face, prominent nose and deep eyes.

Richard D. Bank

I started to let my mind drift to other matters, but once Elie Wiesel began to talk, I became mesmerized with the sound of his voice and then paid attention to what he had to say.

He spoke in a melodic tone, like a fine red blend arising from combining two or more different grapes. In Wiesel's voice there was a Hungarian accent smoothed over by a French cadence, the language in which he wrote, buttressed by the inflection of the Yiddish of his youth, all of which profoundly affected the English he employed to converse with us. But what really struck me, no, more enveloped me, was the depth from which his words arose, coming from some subterranean cavern inside him, something long buried but not forgotten that slowly but resolutely worked its way up and out, expressing a sincerity and simplicity the likes of which I'm not sure I had ever experienced. He had no notes and spoke to us as though he was having a casual conversation with friends and acquaintances. But what he had to say was nothing ordinary. Indeed, the words struck me and have stayed with me ever since.

His book, *Night*, was nothing more than a sustained narrative, he explained, a story, if you will. It wasn't important because it was his story, rather its significance arose from the narrative itself. What was more, he was duty-bound to do two things with the experience he wrote about. He had to remember, and he had to tell. It was as simple as that; although it was only after a decade of silence that he could finally comply with the second part of the mandate which he did mostly by writing than by speaking, so the evening he spent with us was something fairly new to him.

I wish I remember more of that event. Whether there was a Q&A following his talk and if I had asked a question or not; or if given the small size of the audience, he

The Tree of Sorrow

lingered for a time and spoke informally with those remaining; or if I had any direct conversation with him before he or I had left. But I don't recall so I can't say. What I can say is that during the years that followed, I did hear him speak several times more. But the audiences were much larger, much, much larger, and the topics different. Yet his message was always the same: we need to remember and bear witness, which is what he was doing as a teller of tales.

From that night on, I would voraciously read almost all his books and never once was disappointed. In fact, I wrote and published book reviews and review essays on some of his works. I also had the occasion to correspond with Wiesel, and when I wrote asking if he would provide a blurb for my second book, *Why Be Jewish?*, I referred to that night several decades earlier when I first heard him speak. To my surprise, he promptly wrote back and answered in the affirmative. Unfortunately, the galleys reached him just before 9/11, and the ensuing tumult and demands made upon the man who had become a conscience to the world prevented him from providing the blurb in time.

A year after that evening when I first heard Wiesel, I took another course with Professor Friedman called Jewish Existentialism, and in my final paper, "Can God Survive Auschwitz?", I quoted the scene from *Night* where a young boy witnesses another youth being hanged and hears an inmate ask, "Where is God?" After a pause, the man answers his own question with, "Here He is—He has been hanged here, on these gallows." I assumed this rejoinder reflected Wiesel's own belief and perhaps, at the time, it did. But in later years, Wiesel wrote about Jewish sages; he often wore a yarmulke; and he began to speak about religious customs and traditions. All of which made me suspect that

Wiesel no longer believed God had been hung on those gallows. Wiesel's personal theology had little to do with what made him so special to me. Despite becoming a Nobel laureate and arguably one of the most admired people on the planet, he never lost his humility and humanity. For Wiesel, it was always about the memories and stories he had to tell and the simple but eloquent way he imparted them. I could have no better roadmap to follow. While I wish to share some of the things I've seen, some of the people I have met, the milieu in which I lived, and some of the thoughts I have had growing into adulthood in mid-twentieth century America, there is something else, something not easy to discern and even more difficult to convey and yet ever present like a pervasive canopy hovering above and cloaking me in its shadow. But I'll try nonetheless, remembering and telling stories in the best way I can.

Chapter One
The Mansion

My dad didn't build the three-and-a-half-story brownstone where I lived for the first five years of my life. As it turned out, this was an anomaly since, with the exception of that house and the two years I resided with my wife in an apartment when we began our marriage, all the places I have called home were built by my dad. Not that he actually took hammer and nails to the studs and floors or laid the brick or shingled the roofing. He was the "builder" nonetheless who put it all together from the vision he saw for a piece of vacant ground, imagining what type of structures people would want and then creating something out of nothing. But as for the first house I lived in, to which I was taken by my parents, Louis and Ruth Bank, from Doctors Hospital after making my entrance into the world on May 27, 1947, well that was constructed several decades earlier when my dad was just a toddler, so how can he be expected to have built it?

Philadelphia has been described as a city of neighborhoods, and the first one I lived in was Strawberry Mansion, sometimes called The Mansion. There is nothing cryptic about how this name came to be, and the source goes back to colonial times when two palatial homes were erected to nestle in a seemingly boundless park where fields yielded fresh strawberries. One of these estates became known as The Strawberry Mansion and still stands today in what is called Fairmount Park, opposite where I lived on 33rd Street.

Most of Strawberry Mansion consisted of two-story rowhouses, but on some of the blocks near the Park, three-and-a-half-story attached brownstones were inhabited by the very wealthy. However, in a scenario that was to be repeated in later years, these wealthy families took flight to the city's outlying areas as the urban population surged following World War I. By the time I arrived, most of these "mini mansions" had been converted into more affordable residences with each consisting of several apartment units.

Our house, like many of these former mini mansions, had a porch with imposing brown pillars supporting an overhang that allowed us to sit outside in inclement weather or be provided with shade from a scorching sun. The porch led to the first floor comprised of a living room, dining room and a kitchen with an exit to a small rear yard where in the summer, my mother would place me in a big bucket filled with water for me to play and to provide respite from the heat. Our bedrooms and bathroom were on the second floor while the third floor and the top half floor could be let out. My maternal grandparents, Ludwig and Sophie Frank, occupied the third floor, and I would be told many decades later by my mother that the room at the top was rented to a "crazy Polish man." I think by crazy she meant in a mentally ill sort of way. I remember nothing of

The Tree of Sorrow

this man, but I have always had a vision of venturing up a dark, narrow stairway all by myself to that top floor and a closed door. After that, the memory vanishes. It might not be far-fetched to suppose something was repressed, but it would be speculation at best.

Before the brownstone in Strawberry Mansion, my parents resided in a four-story structure a block away called the Park Lane Apartments. The building had once represented luxury living, but by the time my parents lived there, like the rest of The Mansion, its best days were in the past. Nonetheless, there remained much to be said about living in The Mansion. For many, its biggest attraction was not Fairmount Park or the convenience of having a trolley depot that provided convenient connections to other sections of the city including the Park Trolley going directly to Woodside Park, the city's premier entertainment and amusement venue. Rather, what drew many to The Mansion was that it was a ghetto; yes, a ghetto and a Jewish one at that. Hard to believe that thousands of people would seek out a ghetto, but this was because its purpose was not in keeping people in but in keeping people out. Or simply put, keeping the Gentiles out and having a safe place for the Jews to live. And being safe, I submit, was a key consideration to the Jewish way of life during the middle decades of the twentieth century. Even more so for my mother, her parents, and ultimately, me.

Returning to the main attractions, even though my family moved from Strawberry Mansion when I was only five, I do remember them very well. Taking the trolley ride to Woodside Park was an adventure in itself, to say nothing of the amusement rides and especially the merry-go-round on which I always picked a stationary horse that did not go up and down—a sign that caution had already become implanted in me. I was mesmerized watching the trolleys enter and depart from the depot and better yet was when my mother would lead me by the hand to board one and place coins in my palm to give to the conductor who wore a uniform and cap. But best of all, there was Fairmount Park which served as the place of some of my fondest memories.

My grandfather, whom I called Opa, would frequently take me to the Park. Despite the fact it was an outing, Opa always dressed properly when going out. This meant wearing a suit, white shirt and tie, and a hat atop his head. While most wore casual attire, Opa never wavered in the formality of his dress, ceding only to a hot summer's day when he would carry his jacket or leave it at home. I sensed this made him stand out as a bit of an oddity and, by association, me with him.

Nonetheless, I was always up for a trip to the Park. Opa and I would take the steps down from our porch, walk to the corner and wait for the traffic-light signal to turn. He'd grasp my hand and squeeze so hard that it sometimes hurt. But I didn't complain. Once the light changed in our favor, he'd look back and forth furtively before cautiously leading me across the intersection, treading carefully as if walking through a minefield which he more than likely did in World War I. Only after we reached the other side did he loosen his grip.

The Park stretched as far as I could see. There was an endless expanse where picnickers spread their blankets and set up lawn chairs so they could read and talk and have lunch. Men, and occasionally a few women, volleyed balls over the nets on the tennis courts. There were swings, seesaws and slides but with a *"Nein,"* and a stern frown on his face, Opa made it clear they were *verboten* to me. My grandfather would clutch me by the collar until we reached the top of a grassy knoll, and he would find a spot where we had it mostly to ourselves.

Then he would smile and let go. I'd take off like a wild pony, bridled only by my grandfather's vigilant gaze.

Eventually, Opa would catch up with me and grasp me with his free hand. His other hand would generally be holding a half-gallon size jug that he'd be carrying as we made our way from the expansive meadow to jagged rocky embankments where people would be coming and going carrying similar containers. In a number of spots, ice-cold spring water spilled out of pipes that had been inserted to catch and direct the flow of water. Opa would fill his jug to the brim and carry it back home to be placed in the refrigerator. Whenever he wanted a drink, he'd simply remove the jug from the fridge and take a swig. It was Opa's water, and for sanitary reasons, no one else was permitted to drink from it. Not many years later though and far removed from the fresh spring water of Fairmount Park, I began the habit of keeping a bottle of water drawn from the spigot in the refrigerator and taking a drink whenever I felt the urge. It's something I still do today, and I suppose it has more to do with Opa than anything else.

I have a small photo taken when I was about three, wearing a bow tie and a sport jacket draped over me, likely for the Jewish high holidays. It was set in Fairmount Park, and I was standing between Oma, my grandmother, and Opa. Opa was looking straight at the camera and holding his pipe between his tightly drawn, thin lips. His blue eyes were barely visible, being shadowed by the brim of his felt hat. I stood with my hands folded and squinting askew in another direction. Oma was in a dark dress and gazing down at me with concern. No one was smiling. I don't remember Oma and Opa laughing or smiling very much, but I could feel their love and also their angst that something might happen to me.

When we weren't in the Park, Opa spent the afternoons sitting on our porch, usually smoking a pipe, and reading *Aufbau*, a newspaper written in German for German-speaking Jews. Sometimes, I'd help him stuff his pipe. When he opted for a cigar, he'd hand me the paper ring that he stripped off the cellophane wrapper, and I'd wear it on my thumb. I spent a lot of time on the porch because our sidewalk ran alongside a very busy 33rd Street and was considered dangerous by my mother and grandparents, what with the cars and trollies clanking on the tracks and all sorts of people bustling about. Should I wander down the steps toward the sidewalk, I'd be kept in check by Oma gripping my shoulder. To keep me occupied, as well as making my porch inviting to kids to come and play with me, my mother would bring my toys out on the porch. It worked in generating playmates but with a catch. I was never quite sure whether any of these kids would have joined me on the porch if it weren't for all the toys at their disposal. Sometimes, I was totally ignored and found myself without even one of my own toys left to play with. Needless to say, this did nothing to assuage my self-image of being different than those around me.

But not all the time did I feel this way. Two of the kids who entertained themselves on my porch did become my friends—Joey and Stevie—and we were like The Three Musketeers, and I mean that literally. I'll explain this but first, some background information.

In 1930, the Robin Hood Dell opened in Fairmount Park, providing an open-air amphitheater with the sounds of music. In addition to those having seats, people would spread out blankets on the verdant hills surrounding the venue and lay gazing at the stars while listening to the Philadelphia Orchestra and popular bands of the time. I do remember lying and rolling about on a blanket or bedsheet spread out on one of the grassy knolls, but it could also have been an occasion when my family, like many others, would be seeking relief out-

The Tree of Sorrow

doors from the discomfort of a sweltering, muggy house. Or, it might have been both.

In any event, an eatery was needed to feed the large crowds, and in response to this, at the end of my block on the corner of 33rd and Dauphin, David and Terry Cherry opened an outdoor café selling hot dogs for a nickel. Improvements were made, and the restaurant grew to include a finished basement with more seating called The Cherry Pit. The menu expanded, offering platters and fishcakes and best of all, something called "glace," which was shaved ice topped with syrup and served in a cone-shaped paper cup. My favorite was cherry, and to this day, I prefer its descendant, the "snowball," over water ice. Candies were also for sale at Cherry's, and my preferred choice was the Three Musketeers bar.

Whenever one of us had a nickel, Joey, Stevie and I would walk to Cherry's and buy a Three Musketeers. First marketed to the public in 1932, this candy bar consisted of three sections of chocolate, strawberry, and vanilla nougat, each swathed in chocolate. Had this been the Three Musketeers bar that Joey, Stevie and I would share, our friendship would likely not have lasted beyond our first purchase. I, for one, only ate chocolate candy bars, and I suspected my two buddies had the same propensity. No doubt, we would have ferociously fought over the lone chocolate part. But fortuitously for us, during World War II, sugar was rationed, and the company making the Three Musketeers eliminated the strawberry and vanilla parts and produced just one chocolate-covered chocolate nougat bar with three sections that could easily be split along lines demarcating identical portions.

What could be fairer? The three of us would enter Cherry's, forgo the glace and place a nickel on the counter, asking for a Three Musketeers. In an instant, we'd be out on the corner, one of us unwrapping the package while the other two stared down at our treasure, and then with a snap of the hands, the bar would present itself in three equal portions. One for Joey, one for Stevie, and one for me. We were, indeed, three musketeers! And would be until we moved away, literally heading in three separate directions.

There were two incidents that occurred on the sidewalk in front of our house, neither of which involved Joey or Stevie but both of which became indelible memories that have remained with me. One of the memories is a happy one, the other is not. The pleasant memory has been preserved in an 8x10 photograph encased in a frame resting on a pedestal upon which my first pair of laminated baby shoes sit. My feet have always been big but likely did not fill the shoes in question, as my mother always purchased clothing and shoes big enough for me "to grow into." I believe more than economy was a factor, and this propensity on her part had to do with a sense of comfort knowing that my clothes would fit long enough in the event new ones could not be easily obtained, likely a byproduct of her having been forced to hastily flee Nazi Germany with not much more than the clothes on her back. But back to the photo.

I'm just about four and perched atop a pony belonging to some shrewd photographer preying upon a parent's inability to deny their child the opportunity to be donned in a cowboy hat, kerchief, gun and holster and then plopped upon a leather saddle to sit astride a real live horse. It was one of the most exciting and joyous moments of my young life in spite of being more than a few feet off the ground, which would normally leave me frozen in fear—a portent of the mild case of acrophobia that would accompany me the remainder of my life. Yet, straddling the pony I felt comfortable and secure holding the holstered toy gun with one hand and gripping the saddle horn with

The Tree of Sorrow

the other. I had no fear whatsoever of the pony and in fact always maintained a fondness for horses in contrast to my wariness toward most other animals. I'm smiling broadly in the picture and smiling back as I look upon it now.

The second incident embedded in my memory that occurred on the sidewalk in front of my house was quite the opposite of the former and far from agreeable. I recall feeling terrified and howling and thrashing as I was being pulled at the arm by a huge woman who was trying to shove me into the backseat of a car. The reason I was scared had to do with the events that occurred twenty-four hours earlier, when I reluctantly accompanied the same woman into her car to attend my first day of nursery school.

That preceding morning, I was apprehensive being separated from my home and family to be left on my own. But this was soon overcome by all the toys and games and friendly faces of my schoolmates. I remember playing and enjoying myself and didn't even mind having to take a break for milk that was provided in individual cartons for each child. Nor was I concerned when the boy next to me spilt his milk all over the floor. But when the woman in charge noticed the puddle of milk and glared at the two of us demanding to know who was responsible, I couldn't get past the lump in my throat while the boy next to me quickly said something to the effect, "It was him, Mother," as he pointed my way. Facing a false charge and defending myself against it was entirely new to me though I managed to stammer something about it not being me who spilled the milk. This had no effect on the scowling woman who grabbed me at the elbow and led me to a corner where I had to sit in a chair facing the wall the rest of the morning until school finally ended and we were driven home.

Richard D. Bank

I have no memory about what transpired between scrambling out of the car when I got home and the twenty hours later when I was crying and struggling against being dragged into the same vehicle. I do believe that I never mentioned anything to my parents about the spilt milk and false accusation and being thrust into the corner with my nose up against the wall, probably because I was too ashamed about any of it. And I can well imagine my mother's puzzled expression and the abject fear forming on Oma's face at the thought that I was being forcibly taken to some dangerous place. Swiftly, the panic in Oma's eyes transformed into a glare of resolve that she would allow no such thing. The upshot was that after some words, shouted in German and English, the large lady released me from her grip, and I sprinted toward the porch. The following morning, the car with the mammoth woman did not appear to fetch me, nor did it arrive any morning thereafter. In fact, for the remainder of that school term, I never attended nursery school again and remained home, playing on the porch under the protective watch of Oma and Opa.

Arising from that early experience, two characteristics lodged themselves into my developing personality. First, it made me cautious of anything new and reinforced the aura of foreboding that permeated the home in which I lived. Second, it was perhaps the first time I was accused of committing a wrongdoing of which I was innocent. This likely planted the seed which germinated into a sense of justice, or what Oma would later call *gerechtigkeit*, that culminated in my becoming a lawyer.

When I did finally attend nursery school at the age of five, it was not in Strawberry Mansion but in another part of the city, after my family and Stevie's family and Joey's family all moved away to different neighborhoods. In effect, our three families were a microcosm of the di-

The Tree of Sorrow

aspora of the Jewish community of Strawberry Mansion joining up with thousands of other Jewish families from South Philly, North Philly, Logan, Olney and other neighborhoods making the journey to the outer areas of the city and, for some, eventually to the suburbs. What prompted this migration is a good question, and I suspect the main answer is a desire to move on to "the better life" and a peg up the ladder of success in search of the American Dream. But I also remember hearing stories before we moved about Jewish kids getting beat up after school and the need to live in a safer place before I was of school age. Similar tales were repeated throughout the neighborhood, I am sure. It wasn't a question of skin color or a different religion than ours, and I never heard that being said, though I have little doubt it was a factor. In any event, we soon joined the Jews of Strawberry Mansion in the exodus to other sections of the city to form new ghettos where we could feel secure.

I'm not sure if it was Stevie who moved to the Northeast and Joey who moved to the West or the other way around, but I remember visiting each of them at their new homes. In the Northeast, Stevie (or Joey) lived in a typical Philadelphia rowhouse, 16 or 18 feet in width, the kind that was built by the thousands during the late forties and fifties. Joey (or Stevie), on the other hand, lived in a rowhouse in Overbrook Park that had more of a front lawn and was perhaps larger than those in the Northeast; it may even have been a twin, meaning it was semi-detached. My dad began his career as a builder at this time, but he never constructed rowhouses or semi-detached houses—only single-family, detached homes.

Which is what brought my family to the Northwest section of Philadelphia in a neighborhood with fluid boundaries that gave rise to several names: Mount Airy, Cedarbrook and West Oak Lane. Dad had already built and sold several single homes in this area and now was expanding to develop one side of an entire block, not with the customary twenty or thirty rowhouses but with five single homes. He planned on selling four and keeping the fifth for us, and being a businessman, his family would get whichever one was left. As it turned out, that would be the corner lot that no one else had wanted probably because of the higher price.

There were a few older single homes on the other side of the street, but our house stared directly at an empty lot. Across from the side street was an undeveloped area awaiting the completion of a fundraising effort to construct the West Oak Lane Jewish Community Center. To the rear were woods filling the entire back of our block where I spent countless hours exploring and thrashing through the dense shrubbery and broken branches, barely hanging from trees while wearing my coonskin cap and pretending to be Davy Crockett. There were plenty of birds and wild rabbits, and while Davy would have caught and killed one of those rabbits, smacking his lips after cooking the carcass over a fire, I'd cautiously skirt my way around the creature, glancing over my shoulder until leaving it behind.

Our address was 8101 Gilbert Street. Here I would spend the next eight years of my life—in effect, the rest of my childhood.

Chapter Two
Life on Gilbert Street: Part One

When we moved into the ranch house Dad built in Mt. Airy, I had just turned five. When we moved out, I was a "man," or at least that's the case in the eyes of God and Torah, having just become a bar mitzvah. So, I suppose that means I spent most of my childhood growing up on Gilbert Street.

When you entered our brick home from the front porch, you faced a wall with the dining room to the right and the living room to the left. Walking around to the left, you'd pass a stairway leading to the basement; the kitchen was to the right and a bathroom straight ahead. There were three bedrooms: one for my grandparents, the master bedroom and a bathroom for my parents, and the far corner bedroom for me.

Our block consisted of single-family, detached homes and a couple of vacant lots with woods and open areas surrounding us. Most of the other blocks had thirty or so rowhouses on each side of the street which meant that a kid could step out the door and there would be a ton of other kids to play with, but on my block there were only three girls about my age available as playmates. That sucked. As a result, I didn't make any new friends until I started first grade which was more than a year after we moved in because the kindergarten was filled to capacity, and the nursery school I attended instead had mostly younger kids. So, going off to first grade meant a new vista was opening up to me in which I could disappear and be like everyone else and make friends with the other boys like I had with Stevie and Joey. But I was not like everyone else, as I learned one day just a couple of weeks into first grade.

I had just finished lunch at home and was heading back to school when suddenly, the clouds formed a bluish-gray dome, lightning flashed and thunder roared. All the kids sought cover. I was huddled under a maple tree when I felt a tug at my shoulder. I turned and cringed. There was Oma, holding an umbrella over my head and my yellow vinyl raincoat in her other hand. Without a word, she began slipping it on me. I held my arms tight against my side, resisting as best I could, but she was determined.

"Gey vecht!" I shouted, peering around to see if any of the other boys were watching me looking like a sissy while this old woman was forcing my arms into the sleeves of a raincoat. "Gey vecht!" But Oma persisted. I pushed at her and screamed for her to go away. When I turned to make a run for it, my face collided with the ample midsection of my teacher, Miss Schneider. Her eyes burned with the stare reserved for her most unruly students before dispatching them to the stool in the corner of the room. Arms folded across her chest, she stood blocking my escape route.

"Stay where you are, Richard," she commanded. She nodded at my grandmother. I obeyed, and Oma put on my slicker.

"Danke," Oma said to Miss Schneider. Miss Schneider smiled at her. They spoke for a moment in German, and when they parted, Miss Schneider glared down at me over the frames of her horn-rimmed glasses. She clucked her tongue, frowned and ordered me back to school. My head facedown, I scuttled off, not daring to even glance at my teacher or my grandmother.

The buzzer blared from the hallway announcing the start of the afternoon session, but it had little effect on most of us as conversations continued unabated, bodies gesticulated and shoes scraped and screeched on the tiled floor. But then came a clap of the hands and a few harrumphs from Miss Schneider, and the strident students became silent as each and every one of us squared our shoulders and folded our hands, fully focusing on our teacher. Miss Schneider bellowed one last harrumph and then glared right at me, ordering me to the front of the room to stand facing the class. I slouched up to her desk, lowering my beet-red freckled face, wondering what I had done wrong and fearful of what was to become of me.

"Children, learn a lesson from Richard Bank!" Miss Schneider said. "I never want to see any of you do what he did today." There were muffled guffaws and snickers, and the one time I peeked up to see where they were coming from, I saw faces with wide-eyed disdain and shock—especially from the girls. I quickly lowered my head again, staring at my feet glued to the floor as Miss Schneider told everyone about the terrible thing I had done.

"Richard yelled at his grandmother, a refugee from Europe, a woman who was in a concentration camp!" None of us knew about concentration camps, but Miss Schneider made it clear it was a bad place to have been. "We must feel sorry for Richard's unfortunate grandmother. She deserves better than the disrespectful treatment she received from her impudent grandson. You must always respect your elders!" Miss Schneider ended the brief lesson with a grand harrumph.

As punishment, I sat on the stool in the corner of the room during recess for a week. Miss Schneider sat behind her desk peering down at papers, and every so often she'd glance up, cluck her tongue and glower over her horn-rimmed glasses. I was a boy who had been callous and cruel to his poor grandmother. What could be more terrible than that?

Miss Schneider's action affected me in two ways. First, on that day school became a place where I was often anxious, and in anticipation thereof, I would lie in bed at night unable to sleep with pains in my stomach and a fear of the dark. This condition lasted until I was in fifth grade. Second, her conversation with Oma in German reinforced the feeling I had that accompanied every German word my grandparents spoke and every accented English word my mother uttered that there was something profoundly foreign about my family. Despite my hopes to be like all the other kids, I felt out of place and different.

Nowhere was this more evident than at holiday times. How we commemorated these events was quickly ceded by my father to my mother since religious observances were not of much concern to Dad. His own father, long deceased, whose name of David is my middle name, had been for a time a union organizer and always at heart a socialist and agnostic. As for Dad's mother, Celia, she never gave the matter much thought other than insisting he have a traditional bar mitzvah in a synagogue. On the other hand, religion was important for my mother and her parents. Back in Germany, before the Nazis, my grandfather wore a top hat and tails to synagogue on the high holidays, which were celebrated with formal dinners at the estate of Oma's parents where the dining room overflowed with my mother's numerous aunts and uncles and cousins.

The Tree of Sorrow

This stood in stark contrast to the way Jewish holidays were observed in our home on Gilbert Street. For one thing, there was only a small cadre of family members available to join us. After the War, of Oma's eight siblings, only one brother was alive, and he lived in New York and was not married. Likewise, Opa had only one brother who survived the War, and he and his wife traveled to New York to celebrate with their daughter's family. My father had a brother and my mother a sister, with each having only one child.

For my mother's family, the focal point of a Jewish holiday was the service in synagogue. Most of the time, holiday dinner was in the kitchen with a regular meal and everyday dishes. Seated around the kitchen table were my parents, eventually my younger brother, Oma and Opa, and occasionally my mother's sister's family. We dressed as always and conversed sparingly as always. The only exception was Passover, when the seder took place in the dining room. But the ambience was still the same—somber. Religion and God were not to be taken lightly. It wasn't joyous or fun or about a family being together. Rather, it was a matter of devotion, like lighting the Sabbath candles every Friday night and making the blessings over the wine and challah. I couldn't begin to relate to large family dinners such as the ones my wife would recount: her aunts and uncles crammed around the dining room table and her *bubbe* seated at the head; the smell of brisket and chicken soup wafting in the air; all the kids scrambling over themselves to get at the food set out in the living room, leaving them to balance their brimming dishes while sitting cross-legged on the floor and having to shout to get heard over the raucous noises bouncing off the walls. None of this ever happened in my home on Gilbert Street. Not even once.

But it wasn't only the Jewish holidays my family observed in a different way. It was all the others as well. Of course, we didn't celebrate Christmas or have a Christmas tree, but that was the norm in our predominately Jewish neighborhood. But there were other holidays that passed as just an ordinary day in our home that were special for practically everyone else. Take Thanksgiving: the turkey not roasting in the oven, nor an aroma of thick gravy tantalizing the nostrils, nor the slippery feel of biscuits swathed in butter; all were absent from our kitchen table where dinner was indistinguishable from any other night. And why not? My mother and her parents knew nothing of the Pilgrims and the Indians they deceived, and if one wanted to give thanks to the Lord, one did this in the synagogue through prayer.

Other national holidays weren't much different. On July 4th, while flags unfurled from houses and lawns were filled with rows of small flags, a tiny, solitary stars-and-stripes was implanted crookedly on our lawn. As for Memorial Day paying tribute to those in uniform who made the ultimate sacrifice and those surviving veterans squeezed in snugly fitted uniforms marching in parades with throngs of people waving flags and cheering them along the way...well, this was the holiday I dreaded the most.

At school as Memorial Day approached, invariably the teacher would ask the class to raise their hands indicating who had family members who fought in the wars. My father's father, who died from tuberculosis when my Dad was seventeen, had emigrated from Russia before being conscripted into its army where Jews were frequently expected to serve for twenty-five years. My dad was deemed unfit to serve in WWII because he had contracted TB two years after his father passed. I would sit there and hesitate while hands eagerly shot up in the air. Finally, I'd shamefully lift my arm with my hand barely partway up so if called upon, I could mumble something about my hand not being really raised and it was just a mistake. Or I could reply with the truth: "Yes, of course! I have a grandfather who fought in World War I!" It's just that saying so would have been problematic if pressed for specifics.

Should I have shared with the class that my grandfather was a decorated officer, but he served on the other side? Should I tell them that unlike the framed pictures my friends had of their fathers in United States military uniform prominently displayed on shelves and tables in their living rooms, secreted in the corner of a nightstand in my grandmother's bedroom rests a tiny photograph of Opa proudly staring at the camera with his imposing six-foot frame accoutered in German military dress, his lips taut beneath a meticulously trimmed mustache and his similarly attired brother by his side? Must I explain that he was wounded in the War? That his hearing was permanently impaired from the incessant cannon barrages bursting around the trenches? That even with a hearing aid, my mother and grandmother would often shout at him to make themselves understood which I took to mean that they were angry with him? That he suffered from crying spells brought on by damage from the nerve gas he was exposed to that might have been delivered by one of my classmates' grandfathers? That ironically enough because of his valor and injuries, a quarter of a century after WWI he and his wife would not be sent to a death camp but rather to Theresienstadt where old Jews and Jewish war veterans were dispatched to live out the remainder of their days or, if they survived long enough, ultimately be transported to Auschwitz?

Richard D. Bank

No, I would not say any of that. Instead, I'd just keep my arm hanging limply in the air, cocked at the elbow, and be prepared to let it drop at the first sign my teacher was looking my way; praying that if she did happen to notice my semi-outstretched arm, she'd call on someone else who seemed more enthused than me; and all the while my lips would be quivering as I squirmed against the knifelike jabbing inside my gut.

When I was seven, one of the most, if not *the* most, traumatic event of my childhood occurred, and I did not even realize it at the time. I only became fully aware of this thirty-six years later while watching *Avalon*, a Barry Levinson film set in 1950s Baltimore about an extended family comprised of a set of grandparents, parents and a grandson. Armin Mueller-Stahl, the German actor, filled the role of the grandfather who was a Russian-Jewish immigrant, and the grandson was played by Elijah Wood. Like my family, Levinson's cinematic clan had moved from a teeming inner-city neighborhood to a single-family home with spacious surroundings. Continuing with the parallel, Elijah's mother's belly was round and extended, containing a brother or sister soon to be born. The dilemma that was presented at this point in the movie and like the one that confronted my family in our house on Gilbert Street at the time was that the third bedroom needed to be transformed into a nursery for the expectant baby which meant the grandparents had to go.

My eyes were riveted on the movie screen as the scene unfolded. Mueller-Stahl/Grandfather was dressed in gray trousers held up by suspenders that stretched over a short-sleeve white shirt. He wore a straw hat, and he was holding hands with his wife as they made their way down the driveway to the car that would transport them to their new living quarters not terribly far away but far enough that they would no longer be just down the hall from their grandson. With his back to the camera and dressed exactly the way Opa dressed in the summer, including the suspenders, Mueller-Stahl became Opa, and his wife was Oma. Watching this play out, I clenched the armrests of my seat until my knuckles turned crimson. When the car with the grandparents drove off, I turned my head away from my wife so she wouldn't see the tears running down my face while at the same time, I was biting the inside of my cheeks so my sobs wouldn't escape.

I always knew that my grandparents had to vacate our home to make room for my brother. And a couple of decades later while in analysis, I understood how subconsciously I resented my brother for this. But until that moment in the movie theater, I never allowed my emotions to burst through the dam that had bottled them up over the years and feel how terribly sad their moving out had made me.

Of course, at the time, I could console myself that it wasn't as if Oma or Opa had died and I would never see them again. That was delayed for three years, when Opa passed just before I turned ten. I was lying on the living room carpet with my chin resting on my fists, looking up at the TV several feet away when my mother scurried past me pulling my little brother by his arm as she headed out the front door. She said something about Opa being sick and Dad would drive me to the birthday party I had been invited to. It was Dickie's tenth birthday, and I liked being at his house because of all my friends, his parents were the only ones who spoke with an accent like my mother. After the party when Dad picked me up, we didn't drive directly home. "We have a stop to make that won't take long, Richie," Dad said, parking the car. "I'll be right back."

When he returned, he was balancing a tray covered in Saran wrap that I could see was packed with food: lox and bagels and tomatoes and the kind of stuff we ate Sunday mornings, which puzzled me because it was Friday evening. He slid the tray on the backseat. "I have something to tell you, son." Dad didn't look right, and his voice didn't sound right. The lenses of his glasses seemed foggy, and then he said, "Opa died today."

My mother would later say that it was a heart attack, and he had been anxious the previous few weeks because he had to go to the hospital for something or other, and since he didn't speak English, he was afraid that no one would understand him. So, maybe this was a way out for him. After all, my mother said, he had lived a long life at seventy-seven years. But I cried anyway when Dad told me, and he hugged me as I curled into his arms in the front seat of the car with the smell of onions and lox permeating the air.

I didn't go to the funeral because in the Jewish tradition, children should not go to a cemetery. Actually, it's more a matter of superstition. Similar to the custom of washing one's hands after returning from a cemetery to remove the stench of death. The *shiva* for Opa was at our house, and that memory has always remained with me.

The *shiva* begins following the burial of the deceased. Prior to that time, attention is centered upon the body of the departed one, but once that is disposed with, it shifts to the mourners whom friends and family try to console. The more observant Jews "sit *shiva*" for seven days (skipping Sabbath) which is what my mother, her sister and Oma did at our house. They solemnly sat upon hard stools the entire day and evening, and people could come and go through the open front door, bringing food for nourishment so the mourners need not be troubled to cook for themselves. The mourners were clad in dark dresses. Their faces were sorrowful the entire time, but there was no crying, no hysterical outbursts, no hugging while sob-

The Tree of Sorrow

bing, no outward display of emotion other than perhaps a teary eye at most. Such was the German way.

Opa's *shiva* had a lifetime effect on me. On the return from the cemetery, the air of solemnity emanating from the three mourners perched on their stools was like a tiny island in a vast sea swarming with raucous people cramming the living and dining rooms. Scores of hands from outstretched arms balanced paper plates filled with corned beef and roast beef atop slices of rye bread slathered with mustard, and potato salad, coleslaw and pickles; or else, conforming to Kosher requirements, separate dairy plates were packed with whitefish and smoked salmon, slices of Muenster and American cheeses, tomatoes and onions and cucumbers, all to be piled on a mound of cream cheese and swathed in a bagel. Mouths were stuffed with food being masticated as jaws chomped up and down, making the people look like cows except they washed the remains down their gullets with beverages including schnapps, wine or ginger ale as a cacophony boomed through the room with more laughter and guffaws than I can ever remember having heard in my house before.

There is also an image embedded in my memory of the broad, beaming face of a bald-headed man bending down at me. He is smiling, saying something that I no longer recall, and then laughing, he lifts his head and is gone. But his visage lingers and with it my confusion tinged with resentment and even anger that he and everyone else seemed to be so cheerful while Oma and my mother and I were so sad. To this day, funerals and *shiva* houses are meaningless to me, and despite my love for my parents, I never sat *shiva* for either of them, though my heart was filled with loss when they passed.

I don't know the identity of that particular voluminous visage breathing so heavily that I felt his breath like a blast of wind against my face, nor did I know many of the people bustling about that day even though most were family. I know it wasn't Uncle Herman, my father's brother, whose upper lip was covered by a neatly trimmed mustache and who always teased me by pretending to pull the nose from my face and trying to convince me of this by wiggling his thumb protruding from his fingers, claiming it was my nose that was waving at me. Nor was it Uncle Berthold, Opa's younger brother, who was barely taller than me and who always asked me, "Do you know who I am?" and then laughed as I answered red-faced that of course I did. Nor could it have been my "step-grandfather" with his full shock of white hair who I thought was married to Bobbie (the way we pronounced *bubbe*, the Yiddish term for grandmother). Many years later, I learned that though they lived together, they never married, having something to do with Social Security benefits or pensions. I called this expansive man who always seemed to be wearing a double-breasted suit *Zayde* Lyons, while my father and his brother always called him Mr. Lyons. I knew a few others, but for the most part, everyone else was either vaguely familiar or a total stranger. Nonetheless, it wasn't hard to distinguish who was from the Bank family and who belonged to my mother's family. The former were Russian Jews and the latter German Jews, and the two groups could not have been more disparate and sometimes even antagonistic to each other.

Most Russian Jews resented German Jews for their aloofness and failure to help them when escaping oppression as they migrated through or settled in Germany in the late 19th and early 20th centuries. The German Jews responded with their own umbrage that these uneducated people were an embarrassment, often clad in the arcane attire of the Hasidim and conversing only in Yiddish—a bastardization of German that was bound to offend their Gentile neighbors. These uncouth relations threatened to

The Tree of Sorrow

destroy the success and respect it took generations of German Jews to secure in their adopted homeland.

But aside from the mutual distaste the two factions held for each other, there was something in their nature that set them apart. The Bank family hugged and kissed when they met, smiled and laughed, shed tears in public, acted as if they were the closest and best of comrades and would do anything in the world to help each other even though months or years could pass without one making contact with another, and yet they could be unforgiving at a perceived affrontery or slight and then not speak with one another for years or even until death did them part. In different sectors of the *shiva* house where they gathered amongst themselves, arms flayed in the air, backs were slapped, guffaws were heard except when near a mourner, and then out of respect, the boisterous decorum vanished to be replaced with heartfelt expressions of condolences, a touch or even a hug, and possibly more weeping.

As for the Franks and Steinbergers (Opa's and Oma's families), people stood stiffly or sat in chairs with their backs erect. Men were impeccably dressed in starched white shirts with jackets and ties. Formal expressions of condolences were offered with physical contact non-existent except for perhaps a handshake. I could barely hear them when they spoke among themselves. They often just stood or sat in silence while cautiously regarding those around them; there was an expression of sadness that I sensed had more to it than Opa's death—something lasting and permanent. Their empty gazes, the turned-down corners of their mouths, the heavy sighs escaping from their chests—none of these could be explained by the mere fact they were German Jews. There was something more, something else at work at the time that I could not comprehend.

Richard D. Bank

Everyone who was present that day from the Frank and Steinberger clans was a survivor or refugee of the Holocaust, though only my mother's cousin Ernest had been in a death camp. The purplish numbers branded upon his forearm attested to this. He survived Auschwitz, but his little sister did not. Years later, I took Ernest to be a dead ringer for Woody Allen though without the sarcastic wit. I never saw any evidence of humor in Ernest. That had been stolen from him long ago.

Every one of my mother's relatives had loved ones murdered by the Nazis. They lost mothers, fathers, brothers and sisters, uncles and aunts, nieces and nephews, countless cousins, and individually and collectively they carried this burden always. Perhaps their shoulders were erect and squared and their bodies made rigid to resist the weight of the departed placed upon them. No matter how difficult, these people were determined to deny this burden the victory of making them sag and collapse. On the outside, they were stoic; on the inside, I have no idea.

The chasm between these German Jews and Russian Jews was visibly present the first day of Opa's *shiva*, and with few exceptions, one did not speak with the other. Invisible walls were raised in our house, keeping the two groups apart. With one exception. In a corner of the living room where Oma sat on her mourner's stool, alongside her, sitting on a chair, was Bobbie. Though the two women were both of average height, seated on a regular chair, Bobbie towered over Oma perched on the stool no more than a foot from the floor. Bobbie had more flesh on her bones than Oma, but that wasn't saying much since Oma was thin, despite having to inject herself daily to control her diabetes. Ironically, the only time in the previous twenty years she did not inject herself was during her internment in Theresienstadt where insulin was not to be had, but her diabetes was kept in check by the practically sugar-free "diet."

The Tree of Sorrow

Oma wore a simple black dress, and Bobbie wore a plain sky-blue dress. Neither of them was fashion conscious. But there the similarities ended. Oma's hair was dark, and Bobbie's was auburn, much like mine was reddish-brown, and there was still some remnant of freckles on her face, a precursor of the many freckles spread across my cheeks and nose. My dad, whose reddish hair had darkened long ago and now was mostly gone from the top of his head, had said he had freckles, and when he was a kid he'd sit in the sun and drip lemon juice on his face, hoping to make them disappear. If that had worked for him, I would have eagerly done the same.

I stood watching my two grandmothers as they both sat upright with hands folded on their laps and conversing like they were childhood friends, leaning into each other sideways, allowing the words they spoke to draw them closer. How they did this was a mystery to many but in fact was easily explained. Oma spoke German with a smidgen of English, but Bobbie conversed both in English and Yiddish, the latter being a mix of Hebrew, Slavic languages and primarily German. Consequently, the two could more than make themselves understood to each other which for Oma was a blessing since there were few people with whom she could communicate.

Whenever they were together, which was not often, they would engage each other this way. I can't say that Bobbie was a gregarious woman, but smiles and laughter were not foreign to her as was the case with Oma. Yet here and there they both would laugh together and sometimes touch their hands knowingly. What brought on the merriment was always a puzzle to me because I rarely could understand what they were saying. But it made me feel good to see them both happy. To be at ease and comfortable and to feel safe was a fleeting condition for both of them. Certainly for Oma who, like most German Jews, had found herself a prisoner sentenced to death in the country she had called home her entire life. Nor was security anything other than an infrequent visitor to Russian Jews like Bobbie and my long-deceased grandfather, both of whom had taken flight from centuries of persecution to a land of freedom and opportunity that was not without its own prejudices, economic hardships and dangers.

Basking in the tranquil faces of my two grandmothers, I felt at peace. In my home, I felt safe. In my neighborhood and school, where almost all the kids were more or less like me, I did not feel threatened. But there was a world out there, beyond the boundaries of my home and the four or five blocks in each direction, that was foreboding and where danger lurked. I may not have known this in my head, but I sensed it in my bones. This would become clear to me two years later.

Chapter Three[1]
Life on Gilbert Street: Part Two

By the time I reached eleven, the Northwest section of Philadelphia was almost entirely developed. My Mt. Airy neighborhood, consisting predominantly of rowhouses and semi-detached homes, to the best of my knowledge, was 100% white, and nearly everyone was Jewish or Catholic with a sprinkle of Protestants in the mix. Almost all the Catholic kids went to St. Raymond's until high school, while all the Jewish kids went to F.S. Edmonds Elementary School a mere two blocks and a world away. Mostly Catholics lived north and east of St. Raymond's and mostly Jews lived south and west. St. Raymond's took up an entire

---

1   This "currency" featured in the chapter illustration is in fact "pseudo currency" the Nazis circulated in Theresienstadt to deceive the Red Cross and the world that Theresienstadt was a "Jewish City" and Hitler's "gift to the Jews" and not a concentration camp. Sophie Frank took several bills with her after she was liberated.

square block, and the area immediately surrounding the diocese was Catholic turf. Just beyond that locale was a kind of no-man's-land that a Jew traversed warily. This is where I ran into a problem.

I was riding my bike on the way home from a friend's house that was situated in the aforesaid no-man's-land but just across from Vernon Road, a block of commercial stores bustling with people, so I felt relatively safe. Even though I was eleven, it had been only a year since I had learned to ride a bike which had made me one of just a couple of my friends reduced to walking all the time. This is because I received my first bike when I was seven that had been picked out by my mother. It was bright red—a color my mother loved and one I thought "girlish." The bike was also big—very big. I was tall for my age and growing nonstop so, as with the clothes my mother purchased for me, the bike was selected as something I would "grow into." Which meant the seat was high up from the ground, very high up. My friends had 18-inch bikes or, at most, 21-inch bikes; mine was 24 inches and big enough for an adult. In order to mount the bike, someone had to hold it steady for me or else I had to step up on a box to reach the seat. The only way I could touch the pedals with my feet was to have blocks put on them. The few times I rode the bike for any distance were the scariest moments of my young life. The red bike spent the next couple of years in a corner of our garage, and I walked to wherever I had to go.

The bike I was riding on the way back from my friend's house that day was something none of my friends had—an English Racer. It had a light attached to a tiny generator that operated by pedaling so I could ride at night. There were hand brakes to be squeezed instead of using the pedals. There was a gear shift with three gears that made biking easier and more efficient. The color was green—not

The Tree of Sorrow

red; my dad picked out this bike. He knew that red was a girl's color and green was not. And best of all, while it was also 24 inches, I had grown a lot in three years, and I easily mounted my new bike and took to the streets, no longer afraid of falling and smashing my face or worse. Although some caution would have been advisable on the day I was returning from my friend's house near Vernon Rd.

For whatever reason that escapes me now, instead of riding along the block with all the stores filled with people and then cutting down a side street that quickly led to the grounds of F.S. Edmonds, I went straight and biked down a less familiar street that faced Temple University's football stadium which was almost always empty and many miles from Temple's campus. I had barely completed my turn onto that street when I intuitively knew I had a quick decision to make. Up ahead, I saw the blur of three boys on bikes barreling down the road in my direction. I probably had enough time to turn and make it back to Vernon Rd. before they would reach me but that would be the cowardly thing to do should anyone find out. On the other hand, they could just as well pass me by and ignore me altogether. Why should I automatically assume these kids were out to do me harm?

By now, they were well within my sights, and I could see they were about my size which meant they were likely older than me. They appeared to be more concerned with the way they were wildly weaving down the street than with me. Then again, why chance it? But then it was too late. The three of them were upon me and circling me with their bikes, gleefully cackling and shouting things I could not make out. But their intention was clear as they surrounded me, forcing me to stop. I could tell right away they were from St. Raymond's because one of the boys was still wearing his white shirt and tie which was loosened halfway down. Yes, they were St.

Raymond's boys, and I was beginning to fear what was likely to follow.

By nature, I wasn't physically aggressive even though I was tall and husky which sometimes made me a target of other boys so they could prove their prowess by tormenting me or beating me up. In first grade, the class bully would delight in chasing me in the school yard before the morning bell rang and then catch me and sit on me, making us both late for class. We would both be reprimanded, but he didn't care and only smirked while I was ashamed and distraught for repeatedly being the target of Miss Schneider's wrath. After that, I had a few fights like all boys. Some I started and some others started and some just happened. But it was always out of a burst of anger that vanished as quickly as it came; then the fists would stop flailing and the two of us would be friends again, or at least not enemies. But as the three boys tightened the circle around me the way a noose grows taut on a man about to hang from the gallows, I felt a different kind of fear that was foreign to me.

The threesome stopped their guffawing, grew silent and glowered. The look in their eyes seethed with hatred, and their glare was what I imagined the burning fires of hell must look like. The flames seared through me creating a sense of dread as well as confusion. What was it that I ever did to make these guys feel this way about me?

The silence was broken as one of them snickered and pointed at me. The other two followed the line of his sight and started snickering too. What's so funny? I wondered. Their attention was drawn to my right leg that I had stretched out straight to the ground to balance me and my bike. It was jerking and trembling, totally out of control as if it had a life of its own, and there was nothing I could do to stop the spasms. I was literally shaking from fright. I could feel my face flush red.

The Tree of Sorrow

The boys dismounted their bikes, clenched their fists, and snorted their intentions as if I needed that to know what was about to happen. Abruptly they stopped and their fists relaxed. Their faces assumed angelic expressions. I followed the focus of their eyes and turned to see an elderly couple had just rounded the corner and were walking along the sidewalk in our direction. In a moment they would pass and be on their way with their backs to us. I had little time to do something. I dismounted my bike, leaving it to drop to the curb where I deserted it. Stepping away from the three boys, I took up the pace just a couple of feet behind the man and woman and started to follow them up the block. The woman looked back at me a bit puzzled, glanced at the three boys who appeared utterly dumbfounded, and in a kindly voice asked, "Are you all right?" I nodded. She and her husband continued their walk with me still keeping pace until we were a couple of blocks away and I was not far from home.

On that walk making my escape from exactly what I don't know, I was filled with a sense of relief but one that was mitigated and surpassed by shame. Reaching home, I don't think I said much of anything and just planted myself before the TV, awaiting my dad's arrival for dinner. When he came in, I told him what happened. I could tell my dad anything and know he wouldn't yell or scream, and never ever hit me. We'd have "man-to-man" talks in private, usually relaxing on the beds in the master bedroom with the door closed, and he'd listen and tell me about doing the same sorts of things when he was a kid and there was nothing to be embarrassed about. But that day was different.

I don't think we made it to an actual man-to-man talk. I think when he entered the living room, I blurted out something about a gang of boys encircling me and getting ready to kill me and then making my escape.

Richard D. Bank

"And the bike?" He asked. I told him.
"You left the bike?"
"Yes."

The look on Dad's face made me feel worse than the fear I had earlier of the three boys. It wasn't anger. It wasn't shame. It wasn't even disappointment. It was a look of sadness in his blue eyes that hung over me until he led me from the living room and outside to his car where he drove me to where I said I had abandoned my bike. When we arrived, my bike was right where I had left it. The three boys were gone. There was no one else around. My dad loaded the bike in the backseat of the car, and we drove off.

On the way home, Dad said I would have to learn to defend myself. He signed me up at a gym, but that didn't last long since it was not nearby and mostly for adults and older teenagers. He bought me a barbell and dumbbells to lift weights at home which I did religiously and continued to do until I finished law school, when I joined a gym. I did get stronger, and even more, I felt confident that I could handle myself though I almost never got into a fight and avoided physical confrontations whenever possible.

But I do know one thing changed for good. From that day on, whenever confronted with anything resembling the seething stare that felt as if it was blazing through my skin, denouncing me as the killer of Christ or a child of Satan or a parasite on humanity or just a "dirty Jew," I would never ever forsake my bike again, both literally and metaphorically.

Growing up on 33rd Street and later on Gilbert Street meant that being Jewish really wasn't much of a big deal since practically everyone I knew was Jewish. During the Christmas season, if there were satellite photos taken back in the fifties, everything would have been lit up from the multitude of colorful Christmas lights burning brightly except for a patch of black where just a few lights would flicker from my neighborhood. On the Jewish high holidays in the Fall, people accoutered in their finest outfits promenaded on their way to one of the two major synagogues or one of the smaller shuls. A solemnity hung in the air as families found themselves together for the entire day—men not going to work; women not marketing nor doing their chores; kids not going to school nor the playground nor the movies—feeling guilty just watching TV; grandparents and uncles and aunts and cousins making unscheduled visits. On Passover, it wasn't much of a deprivation to abstain from bread and cakes and cookies and even ice cream or anything else that wasn't certified as kosher for the holiday because everyone suffered the same privations. It was only vis-à-vis the Christians with whom I rarely had contact that I ever thought much about being a Jew.

Even attending Hebrew school did little to make me cognizant of the fact that I belonged to a tiny minority of people. I attended Hebrew school at West Oak Lane Jewish Community Center which also served as our synagogue. The rear of the recently constructed building was across the side street from our house while its front faced F.S. Edmonds which made it seem like it was just an extension of the elementary school. But public school and Hebrew school were worlds apart. For one, there were hardly any girls at Hebrew school which made for a good amount of rowdiness. Another difference was that our inhibitions diminished and our desire to learn abated because all of us knew that Hebrew school "didn't count." The grades didn't matter. A note sent home from the teacher that, "Richard isn't doing well learning Hebrew and needs to work harder," didn't prompt my dad to read me the Riot Act and request a meeting with the teacher, unlike the time when I was in seventh grade and I received an E in homeroom, when he ran off in a panic and asked my homeroom teacher, Mr. Tracton, "How can anyone flunk homeroom?" Mr. Tracton responded that most of the boys did because they were very unruly and behaved badly and that I should try harder to improve. I did try harder but still received a D the next marking period. In any event, we all knew that Hebrew school was just a prerequisite to get a bar mitzvah, and no one ever failed to do that.

Nor did the curriculum at Hebrew school and the required attendance at prayer services do much to bolster a Jewish identity. In Hebrew school we were taught how to read Hebrew so we could recite the prayers in the holy tongue, but even with the English translation on the opposite page, we rarely understood a word we were saying. We also were given rudimentary instruction in speaking the language, but other than mastering a few random words, few of us could hold even the simplest conversation in Hebrew. And while we did learn a more comprehensive and updated history of the Jewish people than the stories in the Bible, there was little said about the Holocaust other than it happened. By contrast, the fledgling state of Israel, only a decade in existence, was thrust upon us with fanfare and pride, and in return we pledged our loyalty by singing *Ha Tikvah* to the blue and white flag emblazoned with the Star of David that stood on the auditorium's podium opposite the American flag like the one that we pledged our devotion to daily in regular school.

Preparations for the bar mitzvah began a year in advance when once a week, a brief one-on-one session was held with the man who would help us learn to read our Torah portion directly from the open scroll. This was terrifying. Not the difficult task of reading the archaic Hebrew words lacking vowels which made memorization a necessity, but the old man himself. I don't recall Mr. Something-or-Other's name, but he was unlike anyone

The Tree of Sorrow

else in authority at the synagogue. We didn't address him as Rabbi or Cantor since technically, he was the *shammes*, the sexton or caretaker of the congregation. He was twice the age of our forty-something clergymen who wore dashing suits under their robes. Similarly, he stood apart from the faculty who were mostly public-school teachers in their full-time jobs. Mr. Something-or-Other was different; he was downright scary.

One by one, we'd take our turns entering the small room that might have once been a large storage closet with no windows to open to let out the clouds of smoke that accumulated from the cigarettes the old man smoked incessantly. The student would take a seat right next to the old man who'd be exhaling heavily with a fetid breath while a gnarled hand hovered over the syllables of each word and an extended finger roamed over the Hebrew letters. The finger would pounce on any letter or word said incorrectly or not quickly enough while the student sputtered something…anything…just to make the old man lean back and alleviate the acrid odor of his breathing. All the while, more likely than not, the student would be glancing at the glass pane in the door, seeing the next student awaiting his turn who was making all sorts of faces and contortions to force a laugh, and if a giggle did escape, a smack on the back of the head from the old man's crusty fist would quickly follow. All meaning and sense of importance and accomplishment in becoming a bar mitzvah was lost in that tiny room. Consequently, the only thing that mattered on the day of one's bar mitzvah was getting through the morning service and then being the center of attention at the gala to follow.

And it came to pass that on Saturday morning, May 21, 1960, I was to become a bar mitzvah which literally means "son of the commandment." If it wasn't bad enough getting up extra early, nerves were frayed from the hustle

Richard D. Bank

and bustle in the house, with my parents, my brother and me all vying for the two bathrooms at once and carefully donning the brand-new attire specifically purchased for the occasion while the clock's hands kept creeping closer to the time when the service would begin. Exacerbating the tumult was the presence of a red-haired photographer flashing the sprawling smile of Batman's nemesis, The Joker, while taking "candid" pictures like one of me leaning into a mirror and knotting my tie. What the photo didn't reveal was my frustration with the entire process which proved a mighty challenge for my not-so-nimble fingers; nor did it disclose my intense urge to undo the cursed necktie and wrap it around the photographer's scrawny neck. Barely minutes later, we were directed to pose and force smiles concealing the pressure we were under with so little time remaining before having to dash across the street to the synagogue. My resentment toward this wily little man handling his camera like it was a natural appendage of his arm and flicking burnt bulbs on the floor wherever he went would only intensify later in the evening. But we made it on time and took our seats on the front row of the sanctuary just as the rabbi and cantor ascended to the podium.

Many things of note happened that morning, but most of it was a blur. I followed the advice of the cantor who had said of all the people there, only a handful of old men would know if I made a mistake so if I caught myself doing so, just go right on as though nothing had happened. He also told me to chant the prayers loudly and with confidence, paying no mind to the fact I was a monotone. The sanctuary was packed with four or five hundred people since there were three bar mitzvahs that day. My biggest fear was laughing out loud because one of the other boys becoming a bar mitzvah was Morty, a good friend, who always made me laugh in school and got me in trouble for

The Tree of Sorrow

doing so. But of everything that did happen at the service, only one thing had a major impact on the years to come and I wish it had never occurred.

After I had completed the blessings following my reading of the Torah portion, the rabbi and cantor shook my hand, and the rabbi nodded that I could leave the podium and return to my seat between my parents. As I approached, my mother was beaming and looking beautiful with her dark hair and high cheekbones, accoutered in a stylish dress and a box-shaped hat with a flower ornament. Wearing white gloves, she kept her hands at her side and offered me her cheek which I dutifully kissed like I did every night before going to bed. I was taller than my mother and only had to tilt my head up a bit to look at my six-foot-tall father as we smiled and shook hands awkwardly. We didn't kiss as was our custom every night. That was because now that I was a bar mitzvah, I was no longer a boy. I was a man. And men do not kiss. And men do not hug. This I had learned from observing all the other boys at their bar mitzvahs as they shook hands with their fathers. Almost twenty years would pass before I abandoned this machismo foolishness and I would hug and kiss my father again, after which there wouldn't be an occasion that we didn't kiss each other hello or goodbye up until the day he died.

Some of my friends had luncheons following the service. If it were held at a synagogue, music and photography was generally not permitted. Not much fun. If it were at some other venue, the air was festive with a small band playing a variety of music including rock 'n' roll songs for us kids. And of course, there was the traditional hora that quickly became animated with people holding hands and wheeling in a circle, coming to a stop and stomping feet and clapping hands, or linking arms with someone and then twirling together in the circle's center. For those wanting to make a greater impression, the party became an "affair" held on Saturday night or a Sunday evening at a synagogue's auditorium, catering venue, hotel or a country club that didn't exclude Jews. The affair celebrating my bar mitzvah was unlike any I attended that year. It was held in Center City in the Crystal Ballroom of the Benjamin Franklin Hotel. Couldn't get glitzier than that and one more instance making me feel different.

Why in the main ballroom of one of the most exclusive hotels in Philadelphia? It was a result of one of the few times the self-interests of my parents were in confluence. What motivated my mother was probably subconscious. She had always claimed to have suffered from an inferiority complex, but as I figured out many years later, it was not one she was born with. She was the younger of two children with her sister, Irma, being twelve years her senior, and so she was doted upon by her parents, her grandparents and even Irma, none of whom could resist her beauty and charm. But upon reaching thirteen in 1933, my age on becoming a "man," my mother found herself transformed into a "dirty Jew," ostracized by her former friends, ridiculed by her teachers, and as the only Jew in her class, despised by all the other students. So, as I came to understand it, the need to impress with expensive jewelry and a designer's gown and a gala affair at the city's most prestigious ballroom was a foreseeable reaction to the way she was treated as a teenager.

My father, on the other hand, grew up poor, and for him money held no intrinsic value other than what he could do with it to make certain his offspring would not endure the deprivations he had endured. When he became successful as a real estate developer, he was savvy enough to know the value of maintaining an impressive image and entertaining those he engaged with in business. Consequently, like a rare solar eclipse, my parents' stars were

The Tree of Sorrow

in alignment as they agreed upon the Benjamin Franklin Hotel's Crystal Ballroom to be the venue for my bar mitzvah celebration. Hence, a host of friends, families on both my father's side and mother's side, bankers and brokers, lawyers and politicians, partners and investors, plumbers and electricians, and twenty or so of my friends—all told, upward of two hundred guests—gathered in the ballroom to dance to music played by a twelve-piece orchestra plus a harpist and violinist to provide continuous music during the band's breaks.

Did I enjoy myself that night where I had expected to be the center of attention, permitted to do whatever I wanted but instead found myself emerging from a fog, capable of remembering only fragments of the event? Like wearing a rental tuxedo two sizes too big with an ill-fitting cummerbund covering half my chest; a reception line that went on and on with smiling men shaking my hand and fawning women tweaking my freckled cheeks or planting kisses leaving traces of lipstick; resentfully watching my friends and everyone else stuff themselves with hors d'oeuvres including pigs-in-blankets (kosher of course), and later at the main meal masticating prime rib of beef (also kosher), and enjoying oversized slices from the three-tier cake with thirteen candles that I had blown out, while I was barely able to grab even a fleeting nibble of any of this; the popping of champagne corks, the pouring of sparkling wine by fawning servers wearing white gloves, and the glasses being tilted to awaiting lips by guests affecting postures as if this was something they were quite accustomed to, though for most, it was a rare occasion; the red-haired photographer, back again, making my life miserable, posing me for hundreds of photos knowing there was no way my mother would ever allow a picture from that evening to go unpurchased and be destroyed; making the expectant rounds, visiting each table and appearing surprised and grateful as the men would hand me an envelope containing a check or cash in sums of ten, fifteen or twenty dollars which my mother dutifully recorded the next morning so she would know how generous or not to be when the time came to reciprocate at some occasion.

Yet if all the gifts I received for my bar mitzvah were taken together, they would have paled in comparison to the one gift that, ironically enough, was not presented to me that night. A gift that was bequeathed to me almost a decade earlier by my grandfather and to be given to me on my bar mitzvah. It was left at home, lying in a dresser drawer in my parents' bedroom. I gave it little thought that evening though it would one day become my most cherished possession which I would only part with when my own grandson would become a bar mitzvah. But for now, the story of Opa's gift must wait; I will tell it in due course. After all, this is what I promised to do: to remember and to tell.

Which is not to say the evening went entirely according to plan, for near the end of the night, bursting through the cacophony of raucous conversations and the blare of brass instruments, blasts of firecrackers exploded and ricocheted off the thirty-foot walls of the Crystal Ballroom in the Benjamin Franklin Hotel. The detonations erupted from an adjacent chamber connecting the Crystal Ballroom with the hotel's lobby and where I and most of my friends were exploring the secreted corners, darkened corridors and winding staircase of the vaulted anteroom (the girls were entertaining themselves on the dance floor, having given up gaining any attention from us prepubescent boys).

I did not see the firecrackers ignited, but the repeated cracks and pops were familiar sounds since my dad occasionally brought fireworks home to celebrate July

Fourth. Even before the final explosive volley resounded, I spotted my dad charging into the anteroom, his head revolving around until his furious eyes fixed on me, and he stormed in my direction. I'm not sure I heard all of what he screamed amidst the remaining sizzles and sputters from the firecrackers, but it was quickly clear that I was to blame for bringing them to the hotel and that either I or someone I encouraged had set them off.

But I didn't do it, I said in a stifled voice, fighting back both anger and tears.

Dad's eyes only burned more fiercely. How could I do such a thing at my own bar mitzvah party! Dad spun on his heels and stomped out of the room. A minute later, Jeffrey and Jeff, two of my friends sharing the same name, warily treaded down the stairway, their faces beet red and awash with guilt as they gazed downward, avoiding my teary eyes and accusatory stare. They shuffled off into the ballroom and melted into the crowd as the music played on without interference.

There wasn't much remaining to the festivities that evening when I returned to the ballroom and heard the conductor announce the last dance. Chairs slid away from the tables as guests strolled to the dance floor or began to make their good-byes. Determined to fulfill the promise I had made to myself to dance with Michelle, whose blond hair, blue eyes and French name had enamored me since fifth grade, I pushed aside the image of Dad's disappointment and anger and set out in her direction. Suddenly, a hand clutched my shoulder. I looked up and there he was—the red-haired photographer determined to make me miserable one last time as he escorted me back to the anteroom. Heading over to a sofa, I was set up to pose with a couple of my friends pretending to be exhausted and asleep. It would be the final snapshot in the voluminous photo album of my bar mitzvah. Along with feigning sleep while lying on the sofa, I pretended not to be upset about Dad believing that I had done something wrong that I didn't do. I wanted to prove my innocence; have Jeff and Jeffrey confess to Dad that it was them and I had nothing to do with setting off the firecrackers. But the matter was never spoken of again, though it troubled me for many days. Must have something to do with my sense of *gerechtigkeit*, as Oma would say.

A few months after my bar mitzvah, I had to gather my things and pack those of my possessions that I wanted to take with me to our new home that Dad had just built in a fairly upscale suburb of Philadelphia. I didn't want to move there, and when we were driving home the day he first showed my mother, brother and me the empty lot filled with tall trees and foliage on which he planned to build our next home, I cried in the backseat of the Cadillac Dad had just proudly purchased. Though only a fifteen-minute bike ride from my Mt. Airy neighborhood, I was afraid of losing the friends it took me so long to cultivate and added to that was the fear of not making new ones. At least that's what I said to Dad. But there was also a familiar feeling of anxiety, reminiscent of the way I had felt when we moved from Strawberry Mansion. It wasn't just leaving friends behind but also the loss of a place that was familiar and safe. I was afraid that I would not feel the same in the new world we were entering, which was how I felt in the backseat of Dad's new car as I winced from the stabbing pain in my gut—the same throbbing I had been occasionally experiencing ever since Oma stood over me with the raincoat and Miss Schneider glared at me through her horn-rimmed glasses while her tongue kept clucking away.

"But we're going to have a swimming pool, Richie," Dad said, looking back at me over his shoulder as he was driving and clearly disappointed with my unexpected reaction.

The Tree of Sorrow

"And there's a bedroom for Oma," my mother added with a nervous smile.

A pool? I did love to swim—about the only physical activity I was good at. And there was something comforting about having Oma return to our home and be there all the time. The tears dried as I considered the pros and cons of living in the burbs. When moving day arrived, I willingly went along though with some misgivings which I tried to conceal. One of the items I took with me was Opa's bar mitzvah gift, a watch that had marked time with him when he and Oma had made a move of their own, and like mine, not one of their own choosing. But that is where the similarity stopped. Their journey was into a deep and dark abyss which, according to the hands of the watch, spanned two and a half years.

Chapter Four[2]
The World Isn't Jewish

My new neighborhood was called Wyncote and was situated in Cheltenham Township which consisted mostly of single-family homes on large lots. An adjacent township was Abington, which was larger and more densely populated with a more heterogeneous citizenry. What the two townships did have in common was being subject to a Pennsylvania state law requiring that at least ten verses from the Holy Bible be read at the opening of each school day. About the time my family moved to Wyncote, a man named Edward Schempp, who lived in Abington, took exception to the mandatory Bible reading that his son Ellery had to

---

2   This "currency" featured in the chapter illustration is in fact "pseudo currency" the Nazis circulated in Theresienstadt to deceive the Red Cross and the world that Theresienstadt was a "Jewish City" and Hitler's "gift to the Jews" and not a concentration camp. Sophie Frank took several bills with her after she was liberated.

The Tree of Sorrow

endure and filed a federal lawsuit challenging the legislation. Looking back at this, I'm relieved that Schempp was a Unitarian Universalist and not Jewish, for I cannot imagine how much more difficult that would have made it for me, being a Jew, at my new school.

The case made its way to the U.S. Supreme Court twice. After the Pennsylvania statute was struck down the first time, in an effort to mollify the Court, an exception was made for those who wished to absent themselves from the Bible reading. Needless to say, this did not satisfy Mr. Schempp, nor did it appease the District Court, nor the Supreme Court, and the revised law was struck down as well.

I was blissfully oblivious to these legal goings-on when I took a seat in the homeroom to which I was assigned the first day at my new school, Thomas Williams Junior High, but had I been aware of my right to vacate the room for what was to follow, I would have nevertheless remained glued to my seat, having sense enough to know most everyone would claim seeing tiny horns protruding from my head on my way out. I wasn't taken aback when Mr. Reavy read ten verses from the Bible because I was accustomed to Bible readings in elementary school. But what followed the reading from the scriptures was something altogether different, making me feel I had entered an alternate universe.

Clearing his throat, Mr. Reavy pushed the black-frame glasses up the bridge of his freckled nose, flipped the holy tome shut with a thud, glanced at the class with the innocent smile of a choirboy and said, "Everyone rise." In unison, all the students save one, me, pushed their wooden chairs away from their nicked desks and stood. An instant later, I joined them. Eyeing the class approvingly, Mr. Reavy solemnly spoke.

"Let us now recite the Lord's Prayer."

"Our Father, Who art in Heaven, hallowed be Thy Name...." My ears were filled with words that might as well have been formulated from a foreign tongue. I understood it about as well as I grasped the mishmash of Hebrew chanted during synagogue services. But one thing was clear as I scrutinized the faces in the room and saw everyone's mouth moving in harmony—mine was the only one inert.

But not for long. As if having a life of their own, my lips parted as the sea parted for Moses, and without emitting a sound, my mouth moved about feigning speech. Before that day, I had never heard the Lord's Prayer. The practice of following the required Bible reading with that supplication was unique to Cheltenham, Abington and several other municipalities. In fact, it was the addition of the Lord's Prayer that was cited as a factor in ruling the practice unconstitutional. But again, I was oblivious to the legal proceedings taking place in the federal court system that would soon result in the prohibition of bible readings and prayers in public schools throughout the country. That morning, the start of the first day at my new school, I felt as if I had joined my childhood hero, Flash Gordon, feeling totally disoriented in the midst of a dense haze on the face of an alien planet.

As the class and Mr. Reavy recited the Lord's Prayer and I continued to move my muted lips, I scanned the faces of the students. It was like gazing into a bowl of Cheerios with the perfectly formed beige circles floating in a pond of white milk, all looking identical save for a few idiosyncratic distinctions like hair color or the hue of eyes. But without exception, all lips were moving in unison, forming the same shapes and voicing the same sounds in the same sober tone.

The Tree of Sorrow

Is everyone here Christian? I asked myself. Am I the only Jew in the class? How could my parents do this to me? Are some guys going to lie in wait for me and beat me up after school? Will it be a one-time event or a regimen that I must face daily?

As it turned out, there were half a dozen Jewish kids in my class, but they knew the Lord's Prayer from school and had enough sense to recite it. It also turned out that I wasn't beaten up or otherwise tormented after school that day but not because a few or more thugs didn't bother to hang around following the final bell to ambush me. If they did or didn't, I don't know. It's just that I didn't exactly show up to file through the front portal of the half-century old, gray-stoned two-story edifice situated at the top of a circular driveway that accommodated its five hundred students. Instead, I was being detained elsewhere and not of my own volition.

I wasn't the only new eighth-grade student at the school that September. There must have been another dozen or so, many of whom were Jews whose families made the migration to the burbs. I quickly found myself tethered to one of them whose name was Alan. We were assigned to the same section migrating from room to room throughout the day, following the schedule of designated courses, and since we both had last names beginning with B, we were often seated near each other. Kathy, whose surname also began with a B, wasn't new to the school nor Jewish, but she was part of our section, and from sitting near her, I couldn't help but notice she had blond hair and blue eyes and was very pretty. On the other hand, Alan was heavy, wore glasses, nibbled his fingertips, leaving them crinkly and scarred, and had halitosis. Unlike me, he was outgoing and loquacious and easily ingratiated himself with the more popular classmates, so for the first few weeks, I sort of tugged at his coattails as he weaved his way through the social strata of the eighth grade. On that first day, trouble found me in Mr. White's class where I was sitting in the rear next to Alan.

Mr. White was as indistinguishable as his name suggests. He had a crew cut, an angular nose, thin lips that only on rare occasions parted for a smile let alone discharged a laugh, and he spoke in a serious, coarse voice. He had a thin frame and stood stiffly when not seated at his desk. Mr. White was a no-nonsense guy and that became clear when I heard his voice boom through the room. I looked up from my conversation with Alan and saw Mr. White glaring my way. "You have a detention, Mr. Bank," was all he said, staring straight at me. I had no idea what a "detention" was but found out later it was not that unusual, and it meant reporting to the cafeteria at the end of the day and staying half an hour.

The extra half hour didn't trouble me, but my problem was getting home. We lived just under a mile away which meant no school bus. In the mornings, I was part of a car pool that took several of us to school, but most of the time, the return trip was hoofing it home. When the clearly bored teacher assigned to monitor the recalcitrant students announced the detention was served, everyone scurried out of the cafeteria, down the hall, up some steps, out the main door and splintered off in different directions. All but me, that is. I had hoped but didn't expect that Robert, my next-door neighbor and our rabbi's son, might wait for me as he was to guide me home. But this wasn't so, and I found myself standing at the portico of the school having no idea which way to walk.

I think that was the first time in my life I was alone and truly lost. I had always had a strong sense of place, feeling safe and secure in whatever enclave encapsulated my home, whether it was across from Fairmount Park in Strawberry Mansion or the Jewish part of Mt. Airy. But

The Tree of Sorrow

that day I found myself feeling like one of the space aliens in a movie who escaped from the military base where it had been confined on Earth but had no idea how to return to the planet of its origin. I turned back and gazed at the stone arches atop the massive wooden double doors that had closed behind me and knew there was no way I wanted to re-enter the edifice known as "TW" and ask for help. Shrugging my shoulders and turning away, I drifted down the driveway to the sidewalk that ended at a crossroad. Which way do I choose?

In either direction, there were houses likely about the same age as TW, situated on modestly sized lots. Right or left? I arbitrarily chose right. Wrong. Instead of going a few blocks and reaching Rices Mill Rd., the street on which I lived, and then turning left, I found myself walking half a mile and arriving at a small commercial area with a gas station on one corner, a pharmacy on another and a small bridge to the left going over railroad tracks where a train station was located. I knew going over the bridge would be a mistake, so I turned to the right where I passed several rustic shops, then some larger homes on bigger lots with many trees and green shrubbery, until I finally reached a corner where I recognized a contemporary-style ranch house with a slanted roof and wide window panes that belonged to the parents of Larry, one of the boys in my all-Jewish car pool. It only took a few minutes at lunch talking to Larry to learn he simply had to get A's in every course, and anything less would be a disaster. I shared no such motivation. Years later, I learned that Larry had a nervous breakdown in college and that was the last I heard of him. But that day, Larry's home was a marker guiding me a quarter mile up to Rices Mill Road and our new house, second on the left.

Although I can't say that any one of the 360 or so days that I spent at TW over the following two years would be as unnerving as that first day, this is not meant to imply that I ever felt comfortable in the milieu. In Mt. Airy, my elementary school was built just a year before we arrived, and the junior high was even newer. The buildings were constructed to accommodate a burgeoning populace laying claim to the American Dream and looking forward to a future where they would attain that goal. There was an air of optimism almost everywhere. And why not? It was the fifties. The War was won; the world was safe, putting aside the monthly school drill to scramble under a desk, seeking protection from the atomic bomb the Russian plane might have just dropped in the schoolyard; the economy was growing; and if your parents were only first generation or even immigrants, it didn't matter because almost everyone shared that pedigree. School was crowded; kids were everywhere, galloping like herds of horses through brightly lit corridors where the walls were painted yellow and the frequently buffed tile floors gleamed in green. Stairways were jammed and would clog up when an errant student tried going against the flow. Shouts and laughter and an undercurrent of conversations created a cascade sounding like a raging river crashing off huge rocks along its course. Outside the classroom, and occasionally within as well, school was a noisy and pulsating place.

TW, on the other hand, was anything but. It was staid. Constructed in the early twentieth century, the exterior gray stone walls were like ramparts; inside, the corridors were a dull green and the worn floors either wood or brown tile. Despite the township's wealth, everything was old, and the air smelled musty. Some of the desks in the classrooms were actually bolted to the floor, and rumor had it that in decades past if students misbehaved, they'd be tethered to the desk and stay that way until the end of the day. Here and there, along the walls, dusty frames encased photos of past principals and school superintendents, all old white men staring sternly and demanding obedience. Students and teachers soberly traversed through the hallways with little conversation and even less animation. School was serious business—both for the teachers and most of the students. Which is not to say that students did not socialize. Indeed, there were cliques among the students, though I wasn't included in any one of them unless you count as its own clique those like me whose only commonality was not being accepted by any of the other cliques.

Another thing different about TW from my junior high in Mt. Airy was that there were many activities and programs apart from the classroom. I didn't pay much attention to the baseball, basketball and football teams, but what I did find exciting was the existence of several school dances throughout the year, the first of which was the opening school dance. All school dances took place in the gymnasium and were held on Friday nights—*shabbat*—which sent a message of its own. But our synagogue was no longer across the street prodding my mother to dispatch me to services, and even our rabbi did not compel his son, Robert, to accompany him on Friday night for services when he pulled out of the driveway next door. Indeed, I joined Robert and a couple of his friends as his mother drove us to my first school dance.

We were practically the last to arrive which was generally the case whenever Robert's mother drove us anywhere. She was an artist who had married a lawyer who decided later in life to become a rabbi, and thus she became a "rabbi's wife," a role she was reluctant and unsuited to fill. Nor was punctuality compatible with her artistic temperament as she seemed to be held in place, staring intently at the easel, paintbrush in hand, oblivious to Robert's prodding that it was time to leave.

When we finally arrived, the dance had already started, and the gym was packed with most of the girls wearing skirts and blouses and the boys in ties and jackets. Those not dancing on the gym floor filled the bleachers with the boys standing on one side and the girls on the other side. Most of the undulating figures were girls partnering with other girls doing the jitterbug or occasionally dancing apart as they contorted their bodies in time to the beat of the twist or the hop. Generally, a boy and girl danced together when the occasional slow song was played. Only the most popular and confident boys took to the fast dances, and I was not one of them. So, I stood in the bleachers, arms by my side, gazing out at the gyrating female figures, mulling over in my mind how this was fun.

That was when my eyes, which had been roaming the bleachers on the other side of the room, hit upon Kathy B. staring blankly at the dance floor. She was wearing what she frequently wore to school which made me wonder why she only had two or three outfits. Whenever she was sitting next to me in seats assigned by alphabetical order, I couldn't prevent my eyes from fixating on the tight black skirt rising over her knees and exposing a glimpse of her slender thighs and the white blouse through which either my exceptional eyesight or wanton imagination observed the outlines of a bra. Likewise, that night in the bleachers I couldn't take my eyes off Kathy as I worked up the courage to ask her to join me for the next slow song.

Although likely just a coincidence, that night I believed it was fate that the next slow song was the theme from the movie *Exodus*, depicting Jews who did not meekly trudge into that "good night" but instead fought for their stake of land where they could be safe and proudly live. Seeing that movie and reading the novel had filled me with a

The Tree of Sorrow

sense of self-esteem in being a Jew. Consequently, with shoulders squared and chin struck out, I stepped down from the bleachers on the boys side, made my way through the maze of oscillating teenagers, which parted as did the Red Sea for Moses and the Hebrews, and I found myself at the foot of the girls bleachers with Kathy standing several steps up and staring straight over my head.

"Do you want to dance?" The muffled words fell from my lips to the floor as Kathy continued to gaze above and beyond me without a hint of a response. The crescendo of the *Exodus* song pierced my ears, and I raised my voice. "Do you want to dance?" Kathy's eyes shifted at me as did those of the girls on either side of her. Her lips parted and moved, but I couldn't hear. The girls on each side of Kathy cupped their hands to their mouths and giggled.

"What did you say?"

"No." Kathy was unmoved. Her voice was dispassionate, her face detached, her blue eyes dull and silent. It seemed she couldn't have cared less.

I could feel the familiar burn of a flush wash over my face from cheek to cheek and chin to forehead. I was prone to blush when embarrassed or uncomfortable, and this was amplified by my auburn hair and freckles. Not that I ever saw this, but those around me, both friends and foe, were quick to point this out with laughter. It was something over which I had no control, and that night on the dance floor standing with my head level to Kathy's feet while she hovered several rows of bleachers above was no exception.

Shoulders slumped, I shuffled away, bumping like a buoy off the swiveling torsos that were crashing like waves in the ocean against me until I reached the other side of the gym in humiliation. I slowly stepped up to the midsection of the stands, sliding in between two boys whom I didn't know, and looked off in a blur at the dance floor knowing I would have to remain that way until the last record was played when my mother was scheduled to pick us up.

As one song followed another, I tried to comprehend what had just occurred. How could Kathy have said no? That never happened to me before. What could it be? Perhaps she just didn't like to dance? Or she couldn't dance? Maybe she had a sprained foot? Or she didn't want to hurt her friends' feelings who were left without dance partners? Yes, it must be something like that!

My eyes scanned the dance floor to make sure she wasn't dancing. Suddenly, I spotted Kathy heading right in my direction, making her way through the crowd of teens who had paired off into boy-girl couples as a slow tune wafted through the speakers. Kathy was looking my way. She never appeared more beautiful. She had the blondest hair in the whole room and the bluest eyes as well. My pulse raced. I never danced with a blond-haired blue-eyed girl before except for Michelle, and she was Jewish though her French mother was Catholic but had converted when she married Michelle's father, who had been stationed in France at the end of the War. Kathy would be the first blond-haired, blue-eyed, non-Jewish girl I would have ever danced with. My chest burned with desire and excitement. She was at the foot of the bleachers and staring right at me. Her lips moved. She spoke like an angel.

"D'ya wanna dance?" Of course, I do! Heaven was awaiting me!

I was so excited that I couldn't speak, but I nodded and stepped down to the bench below me.

"Sure," boomed a voice at my back, and I felt an elbow in my midsection forcing me aside as a guy behind me took my place and pushed me over into the boy standing to my right. The guy briefly glanced at me and sneered. I was tall, but he was taller and thin. His greasy, blond hair had the pompadour split down the middle. I recognized him as one of a group of "tough guys" you just didn't want to mess with. He never spoke much, but he did laugh when one of those guys had once asked me why I had big ears and a huge nose. He made his way to Kathy, who smiled. She led him by the hand to the middle of the dance floor where they embraced and moved to the slow rhythm of the song. I wanted to die.

The night my blond, blue-eyed, Gentile dream girl evaporated into a wisp of lust lost in time had its effect on me. It wasn't until eleventh grade that I had the courage to ask out non-Jewish girls—both of them blond and blue-eyed. Every time I left the house to go on one of those dates, I took with me the mortified expression on my mother's face while she mumbled a good-bye as I walked out the door. It was difficult to enjoy myself on those occasions, though I did. But on my return home, seeing my mother still brooding in silence kept me up much of the night. In each instance, I would eventually inform my mother that the brief relationship was over, at which time the weight on my chest was lifted by the sigh of relief and tepid smile my mother sent my way along with a halting movement of her arms, which was the closest thing to a hug my German mother was capable of.

My dad, on the other hand, could have cared less. In fact, his first wife, who died from tuberculosis just two years after they were married, wasn't Jewish. Which may have been one of the reasons my mother didn't want me to know she even existed and something I only discovered by accident when I was in college. But for my mother, marrying someone Jewish was a must, in part so the children would be Jews. This was the obligation the survivors shouldered to the six million murdered, and to ignore it would be to desecrate their memory, though my mother never put it that way in so many words. At the time, this rang true enough, and I soberly agreed to share that responsibility, though I couldn't see how a few dates with a Gentile girl could hurt.

To this day, I still don't know why Kathy did not dance with me. But I cannot dismiss the possibility it might have had something to do with me being a Jew. Most students and faculty harbored no more than the acceptable degree of disdain toward Jews, while those who were avidly anti-Semitic mainly kept it within their own circle of kindred spirits. Once in a while, however, it was as obvious as the nose on one's face, which was the case with Coach K whom I managed to piss off in the early weeks of that first semester.

Coach K was addressed as Coach because no one could pronounce his multi-syllable surname which ended in "-ski." This was the case both on the football field and in the wood shop class he taught. Coach Fry was addressed as Coach or Coach Fry whether it was on the basketball court or baseball field or gym class. Coach Fry was best known for sitting on a chair at the doorway to the shower room, his grayish hair matted from all the moisture, gripping a wrapped-up towel in one hand while he watched the naked boys enter and exit the showers, and arbitrarily, he would snap the towel on the ass cheeks of an unsuspecting lad who would flinch, emit a nervous laugh and speed up to get away. Needless to say, such conduct would not be tolerated today, nor should it have been back then.

On the other hand, Coach K was best known for his bearing; it was overwhelming and awesome. Beneath Coach K's middle-aged blubber was the frame of a forceful football lineman. His square head perched on a thick neck fused into the bulbous shoulders of a thickset body. His voice was gruff. His glare was gruff. His grunts were gruff. The man was just plain gruff. Wood shop was held

The Tree of Sorrow

just twice a week, and on the first day, he instructed Alan B. and me to stand at the front of the class.

"New here?" he grunted. We both nodded. "I'll remember you boys better by giving you nicknames." His eyes narrowed while he sized up Alan. "You I'll call Beauregard," he said. Coach K never explained why, and no one ever asked. But Beauregard stuck, and Alan carried it with him for the next two years at TW. Then he turned to me, and in an instant, he said, "You'll be Fox." He snickered, and again, there was no explanation. I didn't take this as a compliment. To me, a fox was a sneaky, untrustworthy creature, and his choice of this appellation likely reflected his opinion of Jews. But fortunately for me, except for Beauregard and Coach K, no one ever called me Fox.

When the bell rang at the end of class, I heard, "Fox! Come up here." It was Coach K. I sauntered toward his desk. "I want you to come to football practice tomorrow afternoon."

"Not sure I can, Coach."

"Why not?"

"I'll miss my ride."

"You can take the sports bus after practice to get home, Fox." I nodded, knowing it was useless to ask why he wanted me there, and I'd find out soon enough.

Actually, I didn't fully grasp what was in the back of Coach K's mind until looking back upon it almost six decades later. But after a couple of practices consisting of running up and down the field, throwing and receiving blocks, passing and catching balls, each of us received one of two shirts—one designating varsity and the other junior varsity. All seventh and most eighth graders received JV jerseys, and anyone new to the squad received a JV jersey—except me. Despite the fact I couldn't throw or catch the ball very well and I was one of the last to reach the goal posts on the sprints, always huffing and puffing with gut-splitting pain, I was handed a sparkling new varsity jersey by Coach K, accompanied by a mischievous grin spreading across his chunky jowls.

The following practice I was assigned the position of "guard" where I was next to the center and it was my job to push the opposing team's lineman to one side or the other. It was also my job to protect the quarterback from being sacked. We had two quarterbacks, but it was clear who was designated to play all the games. Reggie was tall, muscular, confident and friendly. He was a natural athlete and a coach's dream. Reggie was also Black, the only African American on the team and one of just a handful in the entire school. The day of our first game, Coach K took me aside and gravely said, "Fox, it's your job to make sure Reggie doesn't get sacked. Use your body to protect him like you would protect your own mother from a burglar who just broke into your house. Do whatever it takes, Fox." Coach K smiled a crooked grin and sent me on my way to the field.

I remember almost nothing about that day other than it was my one and only game played on any sports team whatsoever during five years at junior and senior high school. Perhaps I don't recall because I roamed about in a daze, being knocked around and pushed and trampled upon and kicked when down on the ground as spiked feet crashed into my helmeted head. I don't remember if we won or lost or how many times, if any, Reggie was sacked. I do remember that it was a home game and that once the final whistle blew, I staggered into the locker room, got dressed as quickly as possible, keeping my head down and saying little, and walked home determined never to don the shoulder pads and cleated shoes worn by a football guard ever again. By the time I reached home, my plan to extricate myself from this serious dilemma was set in place.

At the end of the next wood shop class, I marched up to Coach K's desk and murmured my predicament.

"Make yourself clear, Fox! You're mumbling. I can't follow you. You're not saying that you're quitting the team, are you? You're not a quitter, are you?" Coach K's eyes narrowed, and he sneered at me.

"I have no choice, Coach. Like I said, I have confirmation classes the same nights of our practices."

"And you can't do both?" Coach K was beginning to see through me.

"I wish I could, but our synagogue is not nearby, and I have to be driven so it means…"

"Your synagogue, eh…. That's a Jew church, isn't it?" I nodded. Coach K muttered something under his breath. He sneered again with a look of disgust and shooed me away with his hefty hand. I turned and made a beeline out of the room, thankful that this worked out. Although, it did come at a price of sorts, as I kept getting D's in wood shop for each reporting period no matter how hard I tried.

I can't say that I felt badly about letting down the team because I hardly knew any of my teammates, and no one ever said much of anything to me. And I figured Reggie would do just fine without having to count on me to protect him. In fact, he went on to be the star quarterback in high school until he was pummeled at a game and taken off the field on a stretcher. He didn't return to playing football again, but he did play baseball. Which didn't work out so bad for him. Thirty-three years after I gave it my all protecting him from storming defensive linemen, Reggie Jackson was inducted into Baseball's Hall of Fame.

And this is where I think I now understand why Coach K put me on varsity football. While I was just beginning to adjust to the fact that the world wasn't

Richard D. Bank

all Jewish, there were a significant number of Jews at TW, and I was already being assured by others that an even larger contingent awaited us in high school. But being Black was something else altogether. There were barely any at TW—just one Black girl in the entire eighth grade. And in some other suburban school districts, there were none at all. Which meant that at most games, Reggie was the only Black person not just on the field, but on the team benches and in the stands as well.

While I realized that much, I did not think this meant someone would want to do him harm. At that point in my life, contact with Negroes (as they were respectfully called) was minimal. Two Black men worked for my Dad on the construction sites—Davey and Ernie—and from the time I began "working" on Saturdays at the age of nine, Davey, Ernie and I got along famously, as they took me in tow. There were a couple of Black housekeepers when we lived on Gilbert Street who came once a week to clean, and they seemed nice enough. But other than Reggie, I never had any interaction with Black students. I had no reason to fear Negroes or hate them and didn't believe they feared or hated me. So even though Reggie was usually the only Black player on the field at games, I couldn't see how this would be a problem for him.

Needless to say, this was wrong. Reggie likely had much to be concerned about from the players on the opposing teams. I can't imagine how many after-whistle kicks were struck and fists smashed into his ribs while bodies were pulled off him. Nor what was hissed into his helmet before he could get himself out from under. But Coach K probably knew about this, and it caused him great concern—not necessarily for any physical or emotional pain suffered by his stellar quarterback but certainly how it might affect the chance for a championship season. Unfortunately, there weren't many volunteers on the squad willing to put themselves between their Black quarterback and the tsunami of snorting linemen who had him in their crosshairs. So, when Coach K saw me that first day in wood shop, tall and big and oblivious of what was in store, he led me like a lamb to the sacrificial altar.

Now, whether the fact I was a Jew had anything to do with my selection, I can't say. But what I can say is that my replacement was quickly chosen the next day, and Beauregard, also Jewish, seized the opportunity to ingratiate himself with the mostly Gentile athletic jocks on the varsity football team when Coach K asked him to take my place. For the rest of the football season, Beauregard implanted his corpulent torso into the turf, absorbing the battering and punishing blitzes by burly lineman hoping to take down TW's star Black quarterback. I'm not sure what he gained from this role, but whatever it was, he could have it.

The rest of that year was relatively uneventful while I floundered like a fish out of its home waters both academically and socially. Making new friends was a gradual process, but on the first day I started ninth grade, something astounding happened in the classroom, striking me like a lightning bolt. This came in the personage of John Cabry, where the C is pronounced like a K, which is the only similarity my ninth-grade history teacher had with Coach K.

Mr. Cabry was of average height, and his compact body was tightly swathed in inexpensive off-the-rack suits that were permanently pressed and just coming into vogue with professionals earning less than staggering salaries. He had a boyish mop of brown hair brushed across his head, and the square, brown glasses balanced on his nose never moved even when his jarring voice blared through the classroom commanding everyone's attention. During the course of that year, without either one of us being conscious of it, Mr. Cabry imbued me with the importance of critical thinking, something I would practice the rest of my life.

I was likely receptive to Mr. Cabry's ruminations because of some things that had been troubling me at the time. It all began in the earliest hours of May 21, 1960—the day of my bar mitzvah though it had nothing to do with my bar mitzvah. That was the day when the architect of the Nazi's Final Solution to the Jewish Question, Adolf Eichmann, was whisked away by Shin Bet and Mossad operatives on an El Al Bristol Britannia that flew him from Argentina to Israel where he would face justice. The trial was held the following year, a verdict was issued that December, and Eichmann was executed in 1962.

In April of 1961 and continuing through August, the trial was held, and during that time, there was extensive media coverage around the world, and I was able to watch it on TV. The attention given to "The Holocaust," the term that was coming into vogue to denote the mass murder of six million Jews, was unprecedented and even with my personal connection to the event, up until then, I knew very little about it, other than it happened. Indeed, the only emotions I had felt up to that point were aroused when reading *Exodus* by Leon Uris and particularly a backstory of one of the characters taking place in the Warsaw Ghetto. As I read those pages, I felt a sense of intense sadness for people I did not know; I felt anger towards the faceless killers, but it was directed into a void; I felt shame that so many Jews appeared to meekly shuffle off to their deaths and pride that there were those who fought back in a battle facing overwhelming odds; and most of all, I wanted to know why. Why did this happen? How could God allow it? What kind of people were capable of committing such heinous acts, slaughtering men, women and children with such barbarity and efficiency? How? Why?

On the TV screen came the answer from Eichmann himself. His high forehead was winning the battle with his receding hairline; ironically, his hawkish nose bore a strong resemblance to the demeaning Nazi caricatures of Jewish men; his face exposed an expression of indifference though at times his lips twisted into a slight sneer; when he spoke it was with dispassion, and it was in this tone of voice that he delivered his defense: he was bound to an oath of loyalty to Hitler; he was "only following orders."

Following orders? This cannot be. How do people do such things? Had they forgotten about the difference between right and wrong? Didn't they think for themselves? Such was my initial struggle with the legacy bequeathed me by the Holocaust, and along with my books, I carried it with me as I began my last year at TW.

Crossing the gray, cobbled threshold and entering TW that fall semester, we were only a year into the new decade which would prove to be tumultuous and even violent and a far cry from the fifties from which we had just emerged. We had been rigorously imbued with the belief that the United States of America was the best country in the world where democracy prevailed, and everyone had an opportunity to attain their dream. "Mother, Flag and Apple Pie," was more than an aphorism, and the addition of, "one nation under God," to the Pledge of Allegiance was taken literally. While that "God" was the Christian god, which needless to say made anyone not Christian feel like an outsider, the values, laws and comportments expected of each citizen were readily accepted by everyone—Christian and non-Christian alike. There was no other way, nothing to think about, nothing to question, and this was the underpinning of the curriculum I had been taught for seven years. And then came Mr. Cabry.

We had a textbook, of course. I don't remember a thing about it. But Mr. Cabry required us to read magazines and newspapers reflecting different perspectives. I found myself reading *Time, Newsweek, The National Review* and some socialist or communist publication which I felt drawn to since it reminded me of my grandfather who died before my birth and who was active in the labor movement. In fact, later in the decade when visiting his brother, my great-uncle, I came upon what I took to be *Reader's Digest*, but on closer examination, it was the premier issue of the English edition of *Sputnik Magazine* made to look like *Reader's Digest* so unsuspecting readers would purchase it by mistake. My great-uncle, Uncle Sam ironically enough, was a subscriber.

Mr. Cabry did not lecture or regurgitate what was in the textbook. In his snug beige or blue suits, a button-down shirt and striped tie, he'd move around the room with alacrity, intently absorbing what any of us had to say and then following up with probing questions, forcing us to think about just what it was we were saying. And of even greater importance, why we were saying it. If a student stated one thing, he'd take the opposing position. If the student changed her mind, he'd change his and argue the other view. There was no winning an argument with Mr. Cabry; there was no losing either, unless you said nothing and just gave up.

It was serendipity that at that time in my life when I needed a weapon to battle those who absolved themselves of the crimes committed upon the Jews of Europe and my family, with the rationale that they were only following orders, I was provided with the armament perfectly suited for the task by my ninth-grade history teacher. Eagerly, I accepted the ordnance as I marched forward unflinchingly examining my own thoughts; challenging, if need be, the thinking of others; and never, never, ever following orders

The Tree of Sorrow

without understanding and respecting their justification. I did so with passion because to do otherwise would acknowledge the rationalization employed to exculpate the perpetrators and collaborators of the Holocaust. I chose this to be my way of saying *kaddish* for the six million.

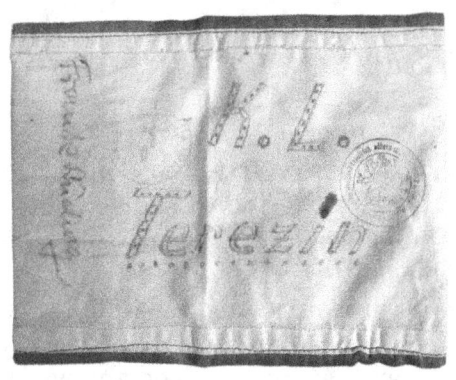

Chapter Five
A Jacket for a Tallit

Although I spent eight years living in Wyncote, I never became more than acclimated to the moderately upscale, sedate suburban community with its tree-lined streets and stone-and-brick houses each sitting like an island in a sea of verdant turf and foliage. Even more, my classmates remained no more than acquaintances—friendly ones at best—and only with one did I retain a friendship through high school. But while there was a subtle demarcation between Jew and Christian in terms of social contact, I can't recall a single overt anti-Semitic act targeted at me by any of my peers. Indeed, it was back in Mt. Airy where I had suffered the debacle of abandoning my bike that the slur of "dirty Jew" was first hurled in my direction.

It was a year after we had moved that I was with my dad driving to his real estate office in Mt. Airy. The car we were in was a beige 1960 Cadillac and the first Caddy he had owned. There were only two American-made cars of status in those days, and to most people, the Caddy beat out the Lincoln Continental in terms of adoration and respect. But my Dad chose a Caddy also because no self-respecting Jew would own a Ford product since Henry Ford had been a rabid anti-Semite. Indeed, for the next forty-five years, Dad drove nothing but Cadillacs except for one time in the eighties when he succumbed to a Lincoln which literally floated away in a flood and was totaled by the insurance company. Like Noah, my dad learned his lesson, and it was back to the Cadillac until the day he died.

Sliding behind the steering wheel of the vehicle, Dad comfortably settled into the cushioned seat and drove with the same degree of unpretentiousness that he always effused. He was no more at home in the Caddy than when he was driving the '49 Chrysler convertible that he took to the construction sites of his housing developments. He'd be wearing worn pants and an open-collar shirt and sometimes boots so the dirt wouldn't ruin his dress shoes. He'd generally wear a felt hat to cover his bald head and if it was cold, a leather jacket to keep him warm. But we weren't in the Chrysler the day I'm thinking about, but rather it was the Caddy, idling at a red light, that the teenagers in the car next to us were staring at.

It was a mild day, so the windows were down in both cars, and the music blasting from the vehicle to our left made it difficult to understand what the boy hanging halfway out the window was shouting. Something about being an old, dirty Jew driving a Jew car that was amplified by jeering and cackling from the other two boys. With the short sleeves of their white undershirts rolled up onto their shoulders and their hair slicked back into "DAs" (duck's ass), they looked like what we called "JDs," meaning juvenile delinquents, emulating James Dean in the movie *Rebel Without a Cause*. When the light changed, the shouting and hooting receded as the car sped off. Abruptly, it veered in front of us, almost clipping the front bumper, forcing Dad to hit the brake.

Sigmund Freud once recounted how one day when he was a young boy, he was walking along the sidewalk with his father when several boys just a few years older than he was flipped the hat off his father's head and sent it rolling into the street. They ran off spewing anti-Semitic slurs as they turned their heads and heckled. Freud watched them disappear and then observed his father quietly step into the street and reclaim his hat, cleaning it off and putting it back on his head. Any anger the young Freud had toward the hooligans in the distance was overwhelmed by feelings of shame over his father. Whatever subconscious feelings of that event became embedded in Freud and the way he seemed to be dismissive of anti-Semitism in the future would be speculative, although it is interesting to note that when psychoanalysis was being tainted as a "Jewish science," in response Freud anointed Carl Jung, the only Christian in his circle, to be his successor. By contrast, my dad responded a bit differently than Freud's father.

Hands clenched the steering wheel. The knuckles on his fist reddened as did his face as Dad floored the gas pedal. I had seen my dad angry many times, but this was different. His jaw jutted out, and behind the lenses of his glasses, his eyes narrowed, staring straight ahead at the speeding car which seemed to be standing still as the distance separating us diminished. The part of Mt. Airy we were driving in was residential with few traffic lights and scattered stop signs so mostly we traversed the streets without impediment. Nearing the commercial area and Dad's office, we slowed down as the car in front with the three teens stopped briefly at a red light just turning green. As the car took off, its muffler rumbled,

The Tree of Sorrow

and a cloud of smoke arose with the fumes assaulting my nose. A couple of the boys looked back at us when the car made a left. They were no longer laughing nor shouting. Their faces bore expressions of apprehension bordering on outright fear. My dad hesitated; his office was in the other direction. He turned right. Dad said nothing. He didn't have to. I didn't feel the same way as Sigmund Freud had.

On the other hand, my mother's response to anti-Semitism was the opposite from Dad's display that day. Actually, not until my mother was into her nineties can I remember her acknowledging ever being subjected to an anti-Semitic slur let alone respond with defiance. My mother, her sister, her parents, assorted cousins and her two uncles were the survivors of the most horrific carnage in human history inflicted upon one species of sapiens by another, and yet, I never heard or witnessed one outburst of anger directed at those responsible by any of them.

Instead of gagging on the guttural sounds emitted when conversing in the language of their persecutors, the German words slipped easily over the lips of my mother's family when they were amongst themselves. At the mere mention of Germans killing Jews, my mother's back would stiffen, accompanied by a tightening of her lips and a glare to her eyes as if a friend had been wrongfully accused of a crime. Nazis murdered Jews; anti-Semites slaughtered Jews; some were Germans; many were others—Poles, Russians, Rumanians, Hungarians and more. Most Germans were not Nazis. They inflicted no harm. What could they be expected to do under the circumstances? My mother and her relations responded in one voice.

My mother and her family were German. The branches on Opa's family tree spanned two centuries with the stump rooted firmly in German soil. Oma's father was respected as an elder in Dorrmoschel, the town in which he lived. On the day he was laid to rest, the mayor attended his funeral and the schools were closed. While the phrase, "German in the street; Jewish in the home," was largely adopted by the Frank and Steinberger clans like most German Jews, that did nothing to prevent the men from wearing top hats and the women donning fashionable apparel as they promenaded to the synagogue to worship on the holy days.

Perhaps one explanation for my maternal kinfolk's restrained response to anti-Semitism lies in a deeply embedded loyalty to a nation and a people of which they were grateful to be a part—albeit not as a wholly equal segment. Possibly the Germans, a civilization steeped in culture, education and law, had a point. Perhaps the Jews in their midst, while tolerated as citizens, were indeed an inferior ilk—something they could not avoid but that was part of their nature as it had evolved over the centuries, beginning with their rejection of Christ and then their cunning ability to survive during the two-thousand-year Diaspora, roaming the far reaches of the world, remaining a blight on humanity. And to some degree, at least unconsciously, the Jews of Germany might have bought into this reasoning.

From when I was a child and well into adolescence, I suffered from what was referred to as an "inferiority complex." Whenever I exhibited some shyness or hesitancy to engage in activities or make new friends, my mother saw this as an opportunity to bond.

"It's just an 'inferiority complex,' Richard. I know. I had it when I was young." She couldn't bring herself to say, "when I lived in Germany." Mother would look at me with a serious expression and sometimes frown. "When I was twelve, no one would play with me." Again, she was unable to explain that it was because she was Jewish and Hitler had just come to power. "I thought there was something wrong with me. But I overcame this by telling my-

The Tree of Sorrow

self that I was just as good as everyone else. And you can too." She'd smile, satisfied she had been of help and that I would be fine.

But there was more to it than that, and there was something else at work which I only became aware of in conversations with my mother during the last two years of her life after her dementia and stubbornness required a transition to the nursing unit of her continuing care community. On most of my visits, weather permitting, we would sit outside on the veranda where a small garden was maintained, possibly reminding my mother of the gardens Oma tended on the grounds of their home in Odenbach. By this time, the malleability of Mother's mind allowed thoughts long buried to worm their way to the surface as she retrieved memories of Germany and spoke of things never said.

I was the only Jew in my class. And in case any of the other students didn't know this, the teacher was quick to remind them of it. Mother's wizened face hardened, resuming the resolve it had brandished for most of her life and the one that I had always been accustomed to.

My best friend was no longer permitted to play with me. The others didn't talk to me. Mother's brown eyes burned deeply. *My piano teacher dismissed me. I had to travel by train to another teacher who wasn't nearly as good.*

Mother's voice was unusually harsh but then tempered as she continued. *When returning from a lesson, I had to walk from the train station to our home. One time, when it was already dark, the town constable who was also the head of the local Nazis came along beside me, smiled and began chatting. He was middle-aged and fat. But I liked his uniform. He started touching me on the arm as we walked. He asked me if I wanted to join him for a date. I was fifteen. I was afraid to say no so I told him I'd have to tell my parents so they wouldn't worry where I was. He walked me the rest of the way home. I told him to wait outside and I'd be right back. I ran into the house and didn't leave until the next day. I didn't tell anyone about it.*

For the first twelve years of her life, my mother was a happy child. She was beautiful, buoyant and carefree. A bright student who loved playing the piano and going to parades, waving to the marching band. She had one sister who was twelve years older, so Mother was raised practically as an only child and relished being the center of attention. Then, everything changed. On the outside, she was still the beauty—high cheekbones, full lips, deeply set, lush brown eyes, thick, black hair that was often parted to the side, leaving a twirl slipping over her forehead. But the luster of her eyes disappeared, and her lips grew taut, leaving no room for a smile. Her voice became quiet and cautious. She'd sit with her shoulders tilted forward and her hands, uncertain where to go, would rest folded on her lap.

Deep down, I think my mother was unable to dismiss the notion that at least some of the things said about the Jews might be true. And why not? She had grown up believing that the Germanic culture and its people were the most civilized in the world. She herself and everyone in her family were proud Germans. The demonization of the Jews by the Germans was like a ball and chain shackled to her mind resulting in acquiescence in the face of anti-Semitism. Unlike my dad, Mother would never have put pedal to the metal in pursuit of the car speeding ahead with its teenage ruffians leaving shouts of "dirty Jew" in its wake. Instead, she would have dutifully set her foot on the pedal, pushing down just far enough to fuel the engine, prodding the car forward at the correct pace. On her face, there would be no trace of hurt, resentment or anger. Her lips would be stiff. Her eyes would be focused straight ahead on the

The Tree of Sorrow

road. Her hands would hold the wheel with just enough firmness to steer it in the correct direction. And we'd be on our way.

Given their respective responses to anti-Semitism, one would expect that my dad would have carried his Jewish identity proudly for all to see and while not with a Jewish star or a mezuzah dangling from a chain around his neck or a yarmulke permanently perched atop his head, then at least in countless other ways. Perhaps casually expressing a Yiddish phrase or word or playing softball on Sundays in a B'nai B'rith league or not working on Saturday and going to Sabbath services instead. But that was not the case. He did none of that. Mother, on the other hand, observed all the holidays. She lit and blessed the Sabbath candles every Friday night, setting the challah on a plate and pouring the wine into shabbat goblets. She'd fast on Yom Kippur, scrupulously observe Pesach dietary requirements and even maintained a strictly kosher household when my grandparents lived with us.

As for me, I never paid much attention to the fact I was a Jew. It was just something I took for granted since almost everyone I knew was Jewish. But with the move to Wyncote, being a Jew involved something that I wasn't. I wasn't like most of those around me. I wasn't Christian. In and of itself, this was not an issue. The question was whether I was just as good as a Christian or must I settle for an inferior role. There wasn't much in my arsenal to make me proud of being a Jew although for a brief span of a few weeks when I was nine, that had been the case.

In 1956, Israel invaded Egypt and in one day overran the entire Sinai Peninsula. The next day, they were joined by English and French forces for the purpose of occupying the area and gaining control of the Suez Canal to insure international shipping. I was absorbed by the events depicted on TV as were my friends. In Hebrew school, we would talk of nothing else. The brave soldiers were all Jews. The blue and white flag they carried to victory was emblazoned with the Star of David and unfurled in the air just like the flag on the podium of our synagogue's auditorium. There was a sense of pride and prowess previously foreign to us that made me and my friends puff our chests and strut with a swagger.

But within weeks, all of this was to change. Led by the United States, the international community compelled Israel, Britain and France to withdraw. President Eisenhower took to the airwaves, his hairless head glistening as he peered over his spherical glasses, and like a stern father, he scolded his wayward children, demanding they behave properly. The errant triumvirate complied. Pride was replaced with humiliation. Power was replaced with impotence.

My pride in being a Jew proved ephemeral and was no more than a distant memory when my family moved to Wyncote, where I warily navigated my way in my new environment. I was uneasy and self-conscious and harbored doubts about my own self-worth. My demeanor stood in sharp contrast to my Jewish classmates, who moved about with an effortless confidence in their step and heads held high. There was an ease in their postures and an assuredness in their voices as they conversed with others regardless of religious identity, ethnicity or race. They were at home, and indeed, for many, that had been the case for several generations. Just as I felt myself to be an alien adrift in a sea of Christian society, I wasn't much more comfortable with my fellow Jews in the suburbs. Not with their stately homes and week-long vacations during Christmas and Easter breaks and eight weeks at overnight camps in the summer and the regal houses of worship where they gathered on the holidays; none of which seemed out of the ordinary to them.

The synagogues in the burbs were different from what I was accustomed to. The one reform and two conservative synagogues loomed along a mile stretch on one side of the main highway in the township. They were lavish, imposing structures; one was even designed by the world-renowned architect Frank Lloyd Wright, with its steeple-like spire stretching several stories toward the sky as if reaching for Heaven. If these edifices were built to impress and intimidate, they succeeded fully, but for me they didn't project what it meant to be a Jew.

I felt different and apart from not just the Gentile world I now resided in but also the Jewish milieu. By the end of eighth grade, I saw little likelihood the situation would ever change, and I believed myself destined for a solitary existence. Then just as things seemed hopeless, an opportunity arose that not only provided a respite from my loneliness and built a bridge back to Mt. Airy but also presented a pathway to express myself as a Jew.

Aleph and *Zadik* are the first and last letters of the Hebrew alphabet. Aleph Zadik Aleph is the name of a Jewish fraternity for boys between the ages of fourteen and eighteen that was founded when fourteen Jewish youths formed the first chapter in May 1924 in Omaha, Nebraska because the Greek high school fraternities would not admit Jews. As soon as I turned fourteen, I managed to convince, cajole and corral enough of my former friends in Mt. Airy and the few new friends I had at TW to start an AZA chapter with myself as president.

That first year had its ups and downs. With all of us in ninth grade, it was hard to persuade the BBG chapters (the female counterpart to AZA, called B'nai B'rith Girls) to schedule "socials" because we were so young, but we managed a few. We also fielded a touch football team, held a cultural activity, attended a religious service, collected toys for the Children's Hospital of Philadelphia and finished the year with almost twenty active alephs.

I couldn't succeed myself, so I decided to run for office at the Council level. I was elected Secretary, and when meeting the other officers, I was pleased to see one was a junior at Cheltenham High School where I would be attending that fall. He informed me of two things: there was only one other aleph at CHS, and whatever I do, don't let it be known I was in AZA.
Why? I asked.
Because it's not allowed. He replied.
By the school?
Yes, it's specifically prohibited.
What would they do if they learned about it?
Don't know. But I wouldn't want to find out.
I had a dilemma. I didn't want to be doing something that could get me in trouble and that I'd have to keep hidden and possibly lie about if discovered. But I wasn't about to drop AZA either. I actually met some cute girls in BBG. So, I did what I would always do when something serious was going on in my life. I talked with my dad.

I hadn't even finished my first week in tenth grade at Cheltenham High School, and I was already causing a stir. Dad, accompanied by Buzz Friedman, the Regional Director of B'nai B'rith Youth Organization, which encompassed AZA & BBG, was scheduled to meet with Dr. Edwin B. Keim, principal, and Wilbur B. Lehman, assistant principal, to discuss the matter at hand. Though the meeting was about me in particular, there was a larger issue at stake. In any event, I wasn't invited to attend.

If I learned anything from Dr. Keim in my three years at CHS, it was that the title Doctor didn't necessarily mean being a medical doctor. It was a term also used to designate those earning a PhD (Doctor of Philosophy), which made Dr. Keim a distinguished persona at CHS since he

The Tree of Sorrow

was the only person in the building we addressed as "Doctor." Dr. Keim had a mild-mannered mien and spoke in a kindly tone. He would lean into a conversation with his shoulders and drop his head so not to appear as tall and imposing as he was. A bespectacled man, he seemed to be always smiling behind his closed mouth. A small, wavy pompadour sat like an island in the front of his head, encircled by a receding hairline with the remainder of his hair brushed back.

Wilbur Lehman couldn't have been more different. His glasses sat tightly on the bridge of his nose. His square head was covered by a crew cut in need of trimming. His jaw was perennially thrust out in defiance as if looking for a fight. The man's wardrobe consisted of ill-fitting sport jackets, white shirts and bow ties. When he looked at you, his glare scorched your chest and seared through your back. Wilbur was the disciplinarian of the school, and no one could be more suited for the task. You never wanted to be summoned to see Wilbur Lehman.

The meeting was held in the office of Dr. Keim where I imagine the plan in place was to play good cop/bad cop which likely came naturally to Dr. Keim and Mr. Lehman. They politely stood and welcomed the two men ushered in. In some ways, Buzz Friedman resembled my dad. He was bald, had a fleshy face, bore a friendly expression, smiled frequently and didn't hesitate to let out a good laugh. On the other hand, he was almost a half-foot shorter than my dad, had his shoes shined and polished, his shirt collar starched, suit pressed and was more diplomatic than my dad. Then again, almost anyone was more diplomatic than my dad. Whether the meeting would reach a peaceful conclusion or be detonated and implode amidst stormy accusations and aspersions would likely depend on who prevailed, the more conciliatory Dr. Keim and Buzz, or Wilbur and my dad.

I waited anxiously at home as the meeting was scheduled for after school hours. I also had to wait until dinnertime since Dad went back to the office before coming home. Whenever I was anxious, I would suffer stabbing pains in my gut. That day was no exception.

I learned from my dad that a grand compromise of sorts was reached. The reason for the ban was that some years back, members of AZA and SAR (Sigma Alpha Rho), the other national Jewish high school fraternity, were accused of creating disturbances at school because of their rivalry. As a result, the prohibition to be a member of either was instituted. I didn't ask Dad if a similar restriction was placed on Gentile fraternities or other youth groups, but I sensed (and later learned) that was not the case. I don't know how Buzz and Dad managed to get Dr. Keim and Wilbur to give any leeway, but they did. The outcome was that I could remain in AZA as long as I did nothing to make it known.

Can I wear my AZA jacket to school? I asked.

No, son. Dad replied.

How about the chapter sweatshirt?

Don't think so.

Can I ask some of my classmates if they would want to join?

Doubt it.

How about asking a girl during lunch if she would want to go to an AZA dance?

Probably not a good idea. Maybe you should just call her on the phone.

Can I talk about it at all with my friends at school?

Dad frowned.

Two years later, I was elected president of Philadelphia Region AZA. There were articles with my photo in the *Philadelphia Jewish Exponent* and the neighborhood weekly paper plus an article in the *Philadelphia Inquirer*.

The Tree of Sorrow

I couldn't tell anyone about it at school. It wouldn't be a part of my record for out-of-school activities. There would be no mention of it made under my yearbook photo. This uniquely Jewish aspect of who I was had to be kept hidden from view, making me feel, at least subconsciously, as if it was something to be ashamed of and if discovered, would have adverse consequences. Something akin, on a much lesser scale, to what my mother and her family had to endure in Nazi Germany about being Jewish.

In effect, the generous concession made by Dr. Keim and Wilbur allowing me to remain in one of the only two non-school organizations (both Jewish) frowned upon by the administration was a precursor to the Don't Ask, Don't Tell policy regarding homosexuals serving in the military several decades later. While I am not equating the gravity of one with the other, I can say it certainly did nothing to make me feel any better about being Jewish in a Gentile world. But despite that, my four years in AZA had a major impact on my development through my adolescence and into adulthood.

Up until the time I joined AZA, everything about being Jewish had to do with the religion. This is how I identified as a Jew. Growing up in the fifties in America, there were three religions: Protestant, Catholic and Jewish. The fact that each had its own denominations made no matter. You were one or another. Being Muslim or Hindu or Buddhist, or atheist, or agnostic or none of the above wasn't considered. But being Jewish was recognized and made you a proper member of American society in spite of some blatant and much latent anti-Semitism.

For me, this meant the Friday night candles my mother hastily lit on the kitchen table which she quickly removed to a countertop before serving the meal. And the wine and challah over which I recited the blessings I had learned in Hebrew school while Dad and my younger brother looked on with distant gazes. It meant a Seder table in the dining room replete with matzah, bitter herbs and saltwater, a hardboiled egg, more wine and placed at each setting was a small Haggadah teeming with pictures and tiny print. At the end of Yom Kippur, we'd rush home from synagogue and charge into the kitchen where the table had been set with empty plates, and we'd be bumping up against each other seeking to withdraw something from the fridge to devour and alleviate the hunger pangs gnawing away in our stomachs. It meant going to Hebrew school twice a week and on Sundays and attending the youth Sabbath services on Saturday mornings until my bar mitzvah. And after I turned thirteen, it meant attending confirmation classes, going to the adult services and removing the tallit and yarmulke from my tallit bag and opening the prayer book and reading the Hebrew, not understanding more than a phrase or two of what I was saying.

The observances of Judaism defined what being Jewish meant to me until AZA presented other ways I could identify as being a Jew that had little or nothing to do with religion. We'd have programs about Jewish culture and history and talk about famous Jews and Israel. We'd collect food for the poor and toys to distribute to children in hospitals because this is what Jews are supposed to do. We had an oratory contest based on the words of the prophet Isaiah, "Saying peace, peace when there is no peace," applying the phrase to a world of wars and violence. Though too young to actively participate, we followed the civil rights movement knowing that surely Jews, of all people, needed to support the call for equality for Black Americans. And after Kennedy was assassinated, I joined my brother alephs to solemnly mark the loss.

When I arrived at a courtyard near the Liberty Bell outside Independence Hall, it was evening, but the lamplights provided ample illumination. I made my way to a podium and stepped up to where a dozen chairs were set. At that time, I was president of one of the councils in Philadelphia Region and was to participate in the program. I wish I could say that I remember the program, but I do not. There were photographs taken, and one of them made the papers. In that photo, I was standing next to the international president of AZA, and together we held a candle. He wore a suit and tie. The others in the photo wore ties and jackets. I wore an open-collar shirt and my AZA jacket. The jacket could be worn inside out. One side was black with the name of our chapter, "William Gerber AZA," in gold letters; if reversed, the color was a shiny gold and the letters were black. That night, I wore the black side of the jacket out in respect for the occasion. This was the jacket I was forbidden to wear at Cheltenham High School.

I'm not sure why I wore the jacket that night. Probably because there was a November chill in the air and also because wearing a sport jacket required a tie, and I hated wearing ties (and still do). But I do know how I felt about wearing that jacket and especially on that occasion. When I slipped my arms through the sleeves of my AZA jacket, lifted the collar up and around my neck and pulled the zipper partway up the front, I felt secure and comfortable within it as if I was sheathed in an invisible coat of armor. I walked with firm steps and my shoulders squared, hoping people would take notice and daring anyone to take offense. I felt Jewish in my jacket in a different way than I did in the tallit that I rarely slung over my shoulders at shul any longer. The tallit made me feel humble as I bowed and davened, reciting prayers I did not understand. Accoutered in my AZA jacket, I was not penitent, I was proud. As the tallit slipped out of my life, my AZA jacket enveloped me even when I no longer wore it.

Chapter Six
"I Was Only Following Orders" – Not

In the late spring of 1963, my world became exponentially larger. Taped to a wall in my bedroom was a picture of a '63 red convertible Corvette Sting Ray with the top down. It was the car that I dreamed about and still do. If my final grade average for tenth grade was a solid B, my dad promised me a car, which would be just about the same time I would turn sixteen and be able to obtain a driver's license. On the last day of school, report cards were distributed, and my heart dropped when scanning the final grades for my majors consisting of three B's and two C's. However, it took no longer than the walk home of a fairly short distance to have conjured a way to transmogrify the grade point average to a solid B and present the case to my dad.

It's like this, Dad, I implored, watching the expression sour on his face as he scrutinized the grades on my report card. *One of those B's is weighted as an A because it is an honor's course.*

Really? Dad's eyebrows grew together as he stared at me.

Yes. Really, I confirmed, trying to sound convincing.

But it's still not a solid B average.

Well, actually, it is.

How so? Dad's eyebrows merged into one dark canopy over his blue eyes.

I have five majors, and you only need to have four majors for the academic track.

Why do you have five?

Pretty much everyone in the academic track does but no matter. What does matter is that for purposes of your class rank, the fifth major doesn't count.

How do they decide which of the five majors doesn't count?

They drop your lowest grade. I stated with growing confidence.

Oh...that seems to make sense.

Yes, and so, my lowest grade was that C in biology which leaves me with an A, two B's, and one C which comes to a solid B average! Dad reluctantly nodded in agreement. It was then I knew I had a future as a lawyer.

I wasn't rewarded with the '63 Corvette Sting Ray, but I was surprised and more than pleased to find a new Chevrolet Corvair in our driveway right around my sixteenth birthday, and it was red and a convertible. Even more, it arrived when school was ending for the summer, providing me with the ability to go wherever and whenever I wanted. As a result, with my horizons seemingly boundless, I would sometimes find myself in places so alien and unnerving that I seemed to be on another planet altogether. Such a place was Ringoes, New Jersey.

Ringoes is a community in Hunterdon County, central New Jersey, and a little less than an hour's drive from where we lived in Wyncote. How I got there is a bit compli-

Richard D. Bank

cated. Every summer since I was thirteen until my second year of law school, I worked either at my dad's real estate office or his mortgage company except for the summer of '63. It was then that Dad and two partners became the new owners of the Hunterdon Drive-In Movie Theater located in rural Ringoes where most of the residents inhabited farms spread sparsely apart. I and my cousin were to work four nights a week with our duties encompassing everything except operating the projector and cooking the hamburgers and hot dogs. Being two years older than me, my cousin appointed himself the "manager," and one of the tasks he assigned me (in addition to cleaning the toilet facilities and retrieving the trash on the grounds), was to collect the money for the tickets.

The drive-in was situated on an open, grassy field bordered by a two-lane highway and cornfields on the other three sides. A small, white stucco building containing the projection booth, restrooms and the concession stand sat in the center of the grounds. Surrounding the building were rows and rows of metal poles supporting audio boxes to transmit the sound of the films. Off in a far corner, aside the dirt road emerging from the highway and leading to the rows for the vehicles to park, was the ticket booth. I would have to get there about half an hour before showtime and remain until after intermission (usually two features were shown). It became one of the most mindless, monotonous and tedious tasks I ever had except for one particular night which I could just as well have done without.

Most nights I would lose the sunlight just before the start of the first feature film and darkness would envelop me. The only light within a hundred-yard radius emanated from the dangling bulb tethered to the ceiling of the ticket booth and another bulb affixed to the frame of the outside door that remained open during my presence.

The Tree of Sorrow

Looming before me was the illuminated movie screen, the semi-lit concession building and the occasional flickering of lights caused by the opening and closing of car doors. Other than intermittent headlights blinking on the highway, everything was pitch black. I could not discern a single cornstalk and only barely hear the whooshing of the cornhusks in a forceful wind or the grunts, squeals and moans of the occasional couple copulating in the cornfield rather than in the confines of a motor vehicle. That night the wind was still, and I heard the cackling of voices and the shuffling of feet along the dirt road even before I saw to whom they belonged.

Sporadic walkers were not unusual, though almost everyone arrived in cars, station wagons with the feet of kids dangling out the rear door window or pick-up trucks likewise packed with children sprawled on the platform. The price of admission was by the vehicle since each only took one space, and the more occupants the better for sales at the concession stand; walkers, however, were charged fifty cents apiece. Walkers often brought blankets or carried chairs which they set up around a speaker. One such group approached that night, without blankets or chairs, and entered the perimeter of the illuminated area around my booth. I wearily grabbed my roll of tickets and stepped outside.

Most of the time walkers were collections of young teenage boys and girls. This crew consisted of four boys about my age whom to me were indistinguishable in appearance: blond hair, tall and thin, angular, pimpled faces, dull eyes and all dressed in blue jeans and white tee-shirts. I ambled over a few feet and almost instantly regretted doing so as one of the boys made his way behind me, blocking my path back to the booth. The other three boys spaced themselves apart, forming a circle around me. The fact they remained silent did nothing to assuage the rumbling in my gut and the difficulty controlling my panicked breathing. I had no idea what they had in mind—whether to rob me, just mess me up a bit, perhaps do nothing at all but buy tickets or possibly "request" free admission, or drag me into the black void of the cornfields, kill me and bury my dismembered body where it was unlikely to ever be found.

Suddenly, the boy directly in front of me and no more than five feet away took a step forward and spoke.

"You a Jew, ain't ya?"

This was different than the incident with the bike in Mt. Airy. Since that time, I had learned more of the Holocaust, and not just in a cerebral sense but in a personal and existential way because many of my great-aunts and great-uncles and countless cousins were murdered. There was no reason to dismiss the possibility that the killing of Jews would continue to occur over and over again, including in places like Ringoes, New Jersey. As the circle tightened around me and I could hear the treading of feet moving forward from the boy behind me, I seriously believed this might be my last moment on earth, and I was scared in a way I had never been scared before.

The question was not repeated; there was no need. Unlike in Mt. Airy when I dismounted my bike, my leg was not shaking. On the other hand, I did not spew back an invective or two which is what I would likely have done a decade in the future. Nor did I speak up and proudly say, "Yes, I am a Jew. What of it?"

What I did was meekly nod in the affirmative. The boy who posed the question drew closer. He stuck his face in mine, and I could feel his breath as he slowly spoke.

"Thought so. Never saw me a Jew before." Turning to his friends, he asked, "Have any of ya ever seen a Jew?" Heads shook in the negative. His lips twisted and his nostrils snorted. Guffaws followed from his comrades.

The Tree of Sorrow

I truly have no memory whether I sold them tickets or not. I do remember breathing much more than a sigh of relief as I watched them meander down the dirt road toward the screen where the first movie was well under way. As the whites of their shirts were swallowed by the darkness, I returned to the ticket booth, closed the door and locked it, not leaving until intermission when the spotlights shone forth from the concession stand, and I made my way warily to the lights.

In juxtaposition to that night, my newly acquired mobility being of legal age to drive a motor vehicle allowed me to discover and explore a world that stood in stark contrast to Ringoes, New Jersey. The Northeast section of Philadelphia, previously only accessible to me by making three circuitous connections of bus routes taking an hour and a half, was now only twenty minutes away, pedal to the metal in my Corvair. The Jewish enclaves in Strawberry Mansion and Mt. Airy paled in comparison to this sprawling Jewish neighborhood. Jews had flocked like geese filling the skies to the Northeast with its newly constructed post-War rowhouses and twins spanning miles and miles. For me, this presented a cornucopia of teenage Jewish girls, any of whom I could date without the guilt of having plunged a dagger into my mother's heart.

The nights I wasn't in Ringoes, I would drive through the streets of Northeast Philly, top down, with a friend or two, ogling the girls sashaying up and down the sidewalks. On one occasion, I pulled over in disbelief as I watched a dozen girls forming a circle and gyrating a hora with feet kicking and arms flailing the air. This was a place where I felt like I belonged.

Sometimes we'd successfully cajole two or three girls to join us for the evening, and they'd hop in the backseat of the Corvair. Other times, I'd have a date and go double with a friend and his date to a movie followed by pizza.

There'd be house parties in the basements of homes where the cinder-block walls were paneled over and brown tile ensconced the concrete flooring. Sometimes these gatherings were "make-out" parties where everyone arrived already paired-up.

As summer drew to a close and I found myself corralled back to the world of Wyncote, I lived for the weekends. There'd be AZA and BBG socials where I could meet girls to date. I never had a real girlfriend nor did I ever go "steady" for even a brief period of time, preferring the excitement of meeting someone new. I'd date several girls concurrently and move on after a short while. I'm not sure why but such was my practice until the fall of '64 and the beginning of my senior year.

It was late on a Sunday afternoon after dropping off my date following an Eagles game that I headed over to Mike's house to hang out for the evening. Mike lived in Mt. Airy, and we had been best friends since first grade though we drifted apart in junior high school. We reunited when he joined my AZA chapter mid-way through the first year. Sitting on the floor of his tiny bedroom and staring at the drawings of sports cars he had sketched taped to the walls, I asked what our plans were for the night.

Want to meet someone? Mike smirked anticipating my response.

Is she pretty? I asked.

Yeah.

Sure. When?

Now. I just have to make a call. Mike lifted himself from the bed and we headed downstairs to use the phone. *But afterward, we have a stop to make,* he added. *You drive.*

It was a pleasant evening, so I had the Corvair's top down. We first went to the house of the girl I was to meet. Mike knew her because she was Frani's cousin, and he

The Tree of Sorrow

knew Frani because he was dating her best friend and they often doubled with Frani and Bruce, a guy in our AZA chapter whom I didn't particularly care for though I wasn't exactly sure why. Frani and Bruce had just broken up. In a heartfelt tone of voice, Bruce explained how unfair it would be to Frani to continue going steady since he was leaving for college. Which of course was bullshit since he was heading off to Penn State, also known as Happy Valley, where hard partying was prioritized over studies, and he likely didn't want to be encumbered. Maybe that's why I didn't care for Bruce. Like Holden Caulfield, I hadn't much time for phonies. I had read *Catcher in the Rye* a year earlier, and it had left its indelible mark upon me. Frani needed cheering up, Mike had said, and she lived just around the block from her cousin so it wouldn't be out of the way.

Most of the time when I headed out to meet a girl or pick up a date, it was in the Jewish quarter of the Northeast, but this time Mike directed me to a neighborhood that was largely Catholic. Frani's cousin was cute and friendly, and we settled in the living room with Mike and her doing most of the talking and me surreptitiously sizing her up. Next day being a school day, we didn't stay long, and I drove around the block telling Mike to make it quick as I parked the car. I vaguely knew Frani since she was in BBG and dating Bruce but had no sentiments for her one way or the other.

Frani opened the front door, gave Mike a big hello and smile, and nodded at me as we entered through a tiny foyer into the living room. Her parents greeted Mike with big smiles and were introduced to me. It took less than a minute for Mike to be convinced to play the piano for everyone which he did with his customary zeal and gusto. Everyone was into the music and enjoying themselves except me. I was totally preoccupied with something else.

Much as I tried, I could not take my eyes off Frani. Even in the relaxed ambiance of her home, she was meticulous in her appearance, wearing a blouse and knee-length skirt; her dark hair was in a flip just touching her shoulders; high cheekbones brought a comportment to her face; dark eyebrows draped her bright brown eyes; she was slim figured and tall for a girl—just the right height for me, right age too—a year younger but also a senior; smart, I had heard; exuding warmth; another sincere smile as Mike and I left....

Instead of taking Mike home, I drove to my house where I had my own phone, and I wanted privacy. I needed Mike to make a call for me. I closed the door to my room.

What's up? Mike asked, sitting down on a chair, lighting up a cigarette and tossing the match in an ashtray on my desk.

I want you to make a phone call.

To who?

Frani. I felt myself blushing.

Why? Mike had a puzzled look. He knew me better than almost anyone and was perplexed at my request, red face and fidgeting.

I want to ask her out, I blurted.

Not her cousin?

No. Mike looked at me long and hard until his face gave way to a smirk and a twinkle in his eyes. Mike was enjoying himself, watching my discomfort until he caught the beginning of an impatient glare in my stare, and he moved on.

Why do you need me to call her?

I could feel the crimson drain from my face as I answered. *I have a feeling she may not like me. I don't know what Bruce has said about me.*

You can't take no for an answer?

The Tree of Sorrow

No. Just call her and see if she'll go out with me. And don't let her know where you're calling from!

Mike did. She said yes. Next day, I called Frani and asked her out. We had our first date on September 19, 1964. I was seventeen. Frani was sixteen. A year later we started Temple University together. We were a couple. We became engaged the end of our sophomore year. On June 23, 1968, we were married and began our lives together. But that is another story. A wonderful story.

Frani and I started going out as we both began our senior year. She had all honors courses at her high school in Philadelphia. My only honors course was in history and called Problems of Democracy. One of the books we read was by Vance Packard, titled *The Hidden Persuaders*, having to do with something termed "motivation research," which was the psychological technique employed by advertisers to figure out how to influence the minds and actions of consumers; something eerily prescient of what's going on in the twenty-first century except that we have "clouds" filled with information gathered by computers from online presence and converted into algorithms that will sway what consumers will buy. By replicating this technique focusing on voters, the threat to democracy is obvious and hence the title of the course.

In any event, in the mid-twentieth century, much of modern psychology was predicated on the theoretical underpinnings of Sigmund Freud and psychoanalysis. Emmanuel Kramer, who taught Problems of Democracy, was well-versed in psychology and Freud. How much of this came from formal studies or the result of personal experience, I do not know. He was middle-aged and not married, and rumor had it that he had once suffered a nervous breakdown, having never fully recovered from the untimely death of his fiancée in a car accident. Mr. Kramer was always fastidiously groomed and his comportment mild mannered. His jet-black hair swathed an oblong face from which his piercing nose prominently protruded. He spoke with a melodious voice and often slipped his glasses up the bridge of his nose whenever he explained the essence of a subject, which in this instance was psychoanalysis.

Freud envisioned three parts to the brain, Mr. Kramer began, sliding his glasses up the bridge of his nose: the id, which was a human being's instinctual nature, engaged in an incessant effort to satisfy the sexual and hunger drives; the superego, serving as the conscience, tried to restrain the id from breaking the rules, generally the products of religion, law, culture, parents and so forth; and the ego, the vigilant intermediary striving to prevent all hell from breaking loose between the two. These constant conflicts and machinations occurred in the brain's subterranean level that Freud called the Unconscious. The best way for an individual to be aware of what was going on in his or her Unconscious and be the "master of his or her house," so to speak, was through psychoanalysis which relied mostly on dream interpretation and free association.

Emmanuel Kramer never had an inkling that he sowed the seed which would germinate into a prominent part of how I would think and who I would be for the rest of my life. At the time, I didn't have an inkling either. If I did, I would have thanked Emmanuel Kramer for departing from the standard curriculum of the twelfth-grade course by adding something he thought was important. Such is the mettle of a fine teacher, a very fine teacher indeed. While unforgivably overdue, might I say here and now, "Thank you, Mr. Kramer," wherever you are.

Many years beyond high school, I was asked in an interview what book had the most impact upon my life. It was a question that I had never considered before. The works of Freud, Buber, Wiesel, Roth and others flew through my

The Tree of Sorrow

mind. The one book that I settled upon surprised even me: *Catch 22*, by Joseph Heller. Like *Catcher in the Rye*, *Catch 22* was not on the reading list in high school, and I read it on my own.

What appealed to me about the satirical novel was its irreverence, advocation for critical thinking and encouragement to confront authority. Early on in Hebrew school, I had learned that when the "first Jew," Abraham, was a young boy, he questioned why people worshipped the statues of gods after he smashed one to pieces, and I have come to believe this spirit of iconoclasm is the cornerstone of what it means to be a Jew. And so, Heller's protagonist, Yossarian, joined Abraham and Holden to become my triumvirate of role models as I matured into adulthood.

It was not long after watching Eichmann on television spouting his testimony that he was "only following orders," that I began reading *Catch 22*. At the time, I couldn't help envisioning other Germans following orders as well: the townsfolk in Odenbach scorning, demeaning and spewing invectives at the Jews in their midst, whom they had once considered their neighbors, including my mother and grandparents; the German soldiers, both the veterans proud of their previous service and the wide-eyed youths eager to fight for the newly created Third Reich, rounding up Jews in the conquered countries, corralling them into cattle cars and trucks and transporting them to ghettos and concentration camps; the SS men who with supreme proficiency implemented the murder of millions of Jews in diverse and even inventive ways.

I was fifteen when I read *Catch 22*, and Yossarian's quandary about how to get out of the military was the farthest thing from my mind. But upon reaching my eighteenth birthday, it became a reality. Although I was still unable to purchase or consume alcoholic beverages and remained ineligible to vote, I was granted the dubious privilege of joining one of the branches of the military and serving my country without the need to obtain parental consent. In the event I was not so inclined, which I was not, I was required to register for the draft should my services be needed in the future.

The local draft board was housed in a small, one-story, pallid stucco structure swaddled in a residential neighborhood bordered by several blocks of commercial establishments. The only feature distinguishing the building from those around it were the numerals indicating the address that confirmed it was home to the Selective Service. It was there that I filled out the requisite form which I handed back to the white-haired lady who wearily informed me that I would receive my status in the mail.

Vietnam was just becoming a growing concern in the spring of 1965 and hadn't yet developed the insatiable appetite for young male fodder that it would in the coming years, but regardless, I was not inclined to spend any time in the army. I thought myself a modern-day Yossarian though with the foresight to know not to get involved with the military in the first place. Fortunately, the 2-S exemption for college students provided a four-year reprieve from confronting the issue.

However, unlike some of my contemporaries, avoiding the draft was not the primary reason I was matriculating at college in the fall. Which is not to say I was looking forward to what I might learn or what might be intellectually challenging. I wanted to be a lawyer, and to do that, I had to go to law school. In order to attend law school, I needed a college degree. It was as simple as that. And so, my next step was college. To be precise, Temple University in Philadelphia where most of my friends from AZA were going. A predominately commuter school with thousands of Jews taking public transportation or driving to the main campus in North Philadelphia. Even before taking a step on its campus, I felt at home.

Chapter Seven
The Meaning of Life: Part One

To say that I sought to matriculate at college only because it was a required stepping-stone to become a lawyer would not be entirely accurate. More and more, I was finding myself questioning just about everything: wearing a tie and jacket to work, to fine restaurants, on a plane, to funerals, to weddings; religious commandments touching every aspect of my life—what I can and can't eat, donning skullcap and tallit when praying, fasting on Yom Kippur, abstaining from anything made from the five major grains during Passover, genuflecting before God and pleading for forgiveness for things I never did while asking that I be granted a fine harvest from seeds I had never sown; and ultimately, beginning to ponder just what is this all about? What am I in the grand scale of things? And just what is the grand scale of things? In other words: What is the Meaning of Life?

In the mid-sixties, this was not an unusual question, and by the end of the decade, it was commonplace to hear it discussed on college campuses and classrooms all across the country, including Temple University where I commenced my studies in the fall of 1965. It was not for nothing that listed on my freshman English Composition syllabus was *The Stranger*, Albert Camus's existential novel about meaninglessness, which I purchased along with other required tomes after standing for hours in a line stretching out of the bookstore and down a sidewalk along a narrow street within the confines of Temple's campus in North Philadelphia.

Temple was founded by a well-known Philadelphia minister, Russell Conwell, who in 1880 was asked by a workingman to tutor him at night. Before long, others requested similar help, and Conwell soon had a steady stream of students. In 1884, along with a staff of volunteer teachers, Conwell received a charter of incorporation for The Temple College to educate academically talented and highly motivated students regardless of their backgrounds or means. When I arrived eight decades later, Temple was a university with numerous graduate programs; law, medical and dental schools; and an undergraduate population exceeding fifteen thousand. The main campus stretched for over half a mile along both sides of Broad Street, the major thoroughfare in the city, and east for several blocks surrounded by rows and rows of attached pre-war homes filled with African Americans.

By the 1950s, with affordable tuition and a non-discriminatory admissions policy, unlike the quota system applied to those of the Hebrew faith still practiced by many top-tier universities, Temple became a cistern for the torrent of a generation of Jews seeking to be the first in their family to attain a higher education. Each weekday morning, thousands of undergrads crammed into subway cars, buses and car pools transporting them to the college's campus where they squeezed through teeming sidewalks and crossed congested streets. Aromas wafted through the air with scents arising from food trucks dispensing pizza slices, hot dogs slathered in mustard and swaddled in relish and sauerkraut, burgers charred black, soaking in spilt blood sizzling on the grill, and from Chinese vendors dishing out egg rolls, chow mien and rice that were not as likely to clog the arteries as the other options.

For the vast majority of students, many of whom had part-time jobs, it was get to campus, attend classes and get out. Indeed, until the new library was opened in my sophomore year, there was hardly a place to hang out even if one wanted to. Except, that is, for the negligible Greek community inhabiting a handful of rowhouses scattered on the borders of the campus. I rushed Alpha Epsilon Pi, one of the two Jewish fraternities, where I knew several of the brothers from AZA. Two things motivated me: to recapture the spirit of camaraderie that I had experienced in AZA, and to have a place where for rush period I could partake in free lunches and avoid the food trucks.

AEPi occupied a three-story brownstone right on Broad Street. At the end of the rush period, I received an invitation to join the pledge class. The orientation meeting was held at night, taking place in the large first-floor room where all those free lunches had been served. The oblong lunch tables were replaced with rows of chairs on which fifty pledges stiffly sat. We were given our pledge beanies, pledge pins, and having been instructed to wear ties and jackets (required to be worn on campus for the entire pledge period), we collectively presented a portrait akin to those hanging in the hallways of elite private schools from which all of us would have been denied admission. Beanies, jackets, ties, shoulders squared, we were fully attentive to the pledge master's speech.

Richard D. Bank

The pledge master spoke with a New York accent, something foreign to the Philly slang permeating the corridors of Temple's buildings. He had black hair and a beak-like nose and reminded me of a vulture. The smile that was permanently spread across his chiseled face when he was promoting the fraternity and exhorting us to join was replaced that night with a scornful scowl. The open hand that had patted our backs when extending a greeting had become clenched with a twisted finger stabbing wildly in the air while he raged about how most of us would never make it through the pledge period because we were not good enough, not real men, not deserving to call the frat members brothers but only Sir or Mister....

I began to tune out and was having misgivings about this pledge thing. Wearing a tie and jacket and a beanie for eight weeks? Saying Sir all the time? Given assignments of senseless tasks to perform? Needing to spend part of every day to attend to any brother's every whim? Not to mention the hazing that we had been promised was not as physical as other fraternities. And...

"Who is Richard Bank?"

I was aroused from my reverie. Could have sworn I heard my name.

"Who is Richard Bank?" The pledge master yelled. I raised my hand. "So, you're Richard Bank?" he smiled. I nodded, thinking he must have heard good things about me from the brothers who knew me from AZA. That I had been president of Philadelphia Region. How happy he was to have me in the pledge class. But his smile screwed into a sneer. "Stand up, Bank! You are one piece of shit, Bank, and I'm going to personally make the next eight weeks hell for you."

He ranted on and on, but I hardly heard what he said. I only saw the stares of the other pledges focused on me. I could feel my face burn red as I endured the expletives,

The Tree of Sorrow

denunciations and loathing all directed my way. Finally, I heard, "Sit down, Bank." And I did. I could feel the sweat dripping from my forehead and my underarms growing wet. The only good thing was that apparently, I was last on the agenda and we were dismissed. I was practically the first one out the door, walking briskly to my car and then driving home, dumbfounded by what had occurred.

Later that night I received a call from one of the senior brothers, a guy everyone called Pop Warner after the famous football coach. He was heavyset and slovenly with a friendly grin and penetrating eyes. He had heard what happened and hoped it wouldn't dissuade me from pledging. He said one of the brothers close to the pledge master had said some nasty things about me. Though he wouldn't name him, I knew it was my nemesis from AZA whom I had defeated in a council election for president. But that shouldn't matter. No one should treat another person the way the pledge master treated me. What happened to "brotherhood"? What about the opportunity to defend oneself from false accusations? Had we lost all our basic rights by becoming pledges? The pledge master's transformation from being your best friend to your worst nightmare showed him to be a phony. What would Holden Caulfield do? What would Yossarian do?

The following day, after my morning classes, I headed over to the frat house. It was a beautiful fall afternoon, and several brothers were hanging out on the front steps with a few pledges wearing their beanies, ties and jackets, groveling here and there carrying out the commands barked at them. I ignored the stares as I made my way up the steps and into the massive living room where all the chairs from the night before were gone. Some tables were set up in the back for the brothers having lunch where pledges were serving their food. Threadbare chairs and sofas filled the front area, and Pop Warner was sprawled on one of them. I caught his eye and walked over. He said nothing and looked at me. I wasn't wearing a tie and jacket.

I handed my beanie and pledge pin to Pop Warner who reluctantly took them. I said good-bye, turned and walked out. I felt as if a concrete slab had been lifted from my chest as I easily breathed in the autumn air. A distraction had just been removed from learning what life is all about. My political science and English comp classes were getting me to think differently, and I was stimulated by the readings and enjoyed the writing. In fact, by the end of that semester, if not for a fortuitous event, my path toward becoming a lawyer might well have been diverted to something entirely different. It came about with the semester's last assignment in my English Comp class.

As Mr. Cohen, the instructor for English Comp I, ambled about the room returning our marked-up and graded blue books containing our first assignment, he solemnly informed us that the grades likely would not be what we expected as they consisted mostly of D's and F's. But not to be discouraged, he said, radiating an air of assurance while continuing to return blue books to the ashen-faced students; most of us would improve markedly as a result of his instruction over the next three months. When the willowy little man dropped the blue book on my desk without as much as a glance, and I flipped it open to see the D grade, I took little solace in his half-hearted attempt to assuage our apprehension at the possibility of flunking the required course.

The process was predictable. Each week, we'd be given a topic and have to write a three- to five-page essay on the subject. Each week, the dark-haired, diminutive Mr. Cohen, accoutered in affordable corduroy suits, multi-colored flannel shirts and clashing plaid ties, would return the blue books; and as the weeks went by, the grades, as he foretold, went up. I really didn't see much difference in my writing from the first piece to the penultimate piece where I received a B+, but I did begin to understand the meaning of a self-fulfilling prophesy. Clearly, this was Mr. Cohen's modus operandi to prove his proficiency as an instructor while working toward his PhD.

With two weeks remaining of classes, Mr. Cohen announced that we could write anything we wanted for the last essay. Many of the students groaned, not thrilled with the burden of picking a subject. But not me. I knew right away what I would write about. After all, I was searching for the meaning of life, and here was an opportunity to actually put my musings down on paper. And that is exactly what I did.

I wrote about the inconsequentiality of us Homo sapiens in the greater scheme of things. How small we are compared to the immenseness of the cosmos. How shallow we are in contrast with the depths of the seas. How the span of our lives is barely a blink in eternity. How we are but a speck in the vastness of the universe. And so on.

The next week, I handed in my essay. The week after that, at the end of the last class, Mr. Cohen returned our assignments. He dropped the blue book on my desk though this time he did so with an unaccustomed glance and walked off. I tucked the blue book between my textbooks and left. Once in the hallway, I anxiously opened the blue book, flipped to the last page, and saw an A boldly penned in red. Also written in red was a comment to the effect that Mr. Cohen wanted to talk to me about the essay and could I see him in his office anytime Thursday morning during the week-long semester break in January.

I was looking forward to sleeping late during the hiatus between semesters, but my curiosity was more than piqued by Mr. Cohen's invitation. Could it be that perhaps he saw in me the makings of a talented writer? In the days leading up to the meeting, I began to fancy myself in my writer's garret, typewriter in front of me, a glass of scotch over ice on the left hand side of the desk and the embers of a burning cigarette dangling over an ash tray to the right while I closed my eyes, straining to visualize the opening scene of the great American novel I was to pen. This and more I would be encouraged to do by Mr. Cohen as we conversed over Joyce and Hemingway and Steinbeck in his office that upcoming Thursday morning.

What I didn't count on was a snowstorm during the night dumping almost a foot of the white crystal-like flakes by dawn Thursday. Undaunted, I cleared the snow from my car after shoveling the driveway of our Wyncote home and made my way onto the roads. Given some plowing overnight and the fact that my route consisted of main thoroughfares leading to Broad Street, I was able to get to Temple's campus albeit in twice the normal time.

With no classes in session and the severity of the snowstorm, the normally teeming streets and sidewalks of Temple's campus were practically deserted. I was able to park on the one open lot where a section had been plowed clear. Other than narrow swathes recently shoveled, the campus was one thick blanket of snow with solitary figures here and there, heads turned down to avoid the blustery wind, snaking their respective ways through the rising drifts. I was beginning to doubt my sanity in undertaking this trip. It was just a couple of blocks to the row of houses in the middle of which the English Department's offices were located. My heart began to sink along with my foot into the undisturbed mound of snow covering the steps leading up to the front door of the apparently deserted two-story brownstone. I turned the knob to no avail and emitted several expletives before knocking on the locked door. Another futile twist on the knob, several more thun-

The Tree of Sorrow

derous strikes on the door and many more expletives later, I resignedly turned away, returning to the parking lot.

On the way home, my anger dissipated along with the plowed piles of snow, stacked against the curbs of the streets, that were melting under the sun's warming rays, and in its stead disappointment set in. I resolved to contact Mr. Cohen the following week and re-schedule our appointment. But I never did. There was a new semester with a new schedule, and I quickly fell into a new routine. I was at Temple to get a degree, go to law school, become a lawyer and change the world. And it was becoming clearer and clearer that Frani and I would be married sooner rather than later and have a family. It was a good plan and one I was happy with. There wasn't time for much else. Even if I had a flair for writing, I didn't want to be a Mr. Cohen teaching English Comp courses while squeezing in the writing on the side. Anyway, I could just as easily find time to write while in school and even later when I was a lawyer. Why not? That's the logical thing to do. That's the safe thing to do. And that's exactly what I did.

Yet, every so often I would wonder what if I had seen Mr. Cohen? Just what was it he would have said? And what would I have done? Would my life have been altered? For better or worse or not much different at all? I would never know, and all because of the fortuitousness of a snowstorm.

In my quest to discover the meaning of life, I enrolled in a course entitled, Religion and Human Life, in the spring semester of my sophomore year. The professor was a man in his mid-thirties named John Raines who had received his master's in divinity and doctorate in theology from the esteemed Union Theological Seminary. He was also an ordained Methodist minister. Not much there to make a Jew like me feel comfortable, and yet, in this most unlikely of situations, by semester's end, while not ascertaining the meaning of life, I did discover what being a Jew really meant—at least to me.

Scuttlebutt was that John Raines had been lured away from the University of Pennsylvania where he taught while pursuing a PhD. It was a rare instance indeed to snag a faculty member of an Ivy to come to a blue-collar school like Temple, so he was endeared to the class at the outset. But even without this, standing over six feet tall with a sturdy frame exuding strength, he radiated a presence that could not be dismissed.

Raines would begin each class planting himself front and center with his arms folded, an unlit cigar firmly set between his thick lips and a square jaw jutting out challenging the world. His shirtsleeves would be rolled up to his elbows as if he were readying himself to dig dirt to plant a garden or a tree. A tie always dangled down his broad chest, stopping just where his white shirt had gathered at his burgeoning paunch. There'd be a glimmer in his eyes every time he began class as his husky voice rocketed off the walls. Whenever he wanted to make a point, he'd raise his cigar as though he was about to hurl a spear that would soar through the air and shatter its target to pieces. Which is what he repeatedly did to the preconceived notions almost all of us held about religion, God, divine entities, rituals, dogmas; indeed, just about anything and everything.

Raines was a nondiscriminatory debunker of any and all religious canons, sparing none nor favoring one over another. After objectively summarizing the doctrine of the religion of the week and our reading assignments on the subject, with a twinkle in his eyes, he'd begin pacing back and forth in the front of the room, waving his unlit cigar like a baton, conducting an invisible orchestra playing heathen music. He did this with the Eastern religions, with Islam, with Chris-

The Tree of Sorrow

tianity and with Judaism which he did with exceptional fervor.

Not that he was anti-Semitic. Quite the contrary. He set his sights upon the golden calf the Hebrews had erected that greeted Moses when he descended from Mt. Sinai bearing the Ten Commandments. And like Moses smashing the tablets on the rocks, Raines did likewise with the false idols and gods and uncontested tenets of Judaism just as he did with all religions. The essence of Judaism, Raines believed, and its singular contribution to humanity began with Abraham, who when a youth, literally shattered the small godlike statues in his father's shop. What Abraham and his descendants bestowed upon the world was something Raines called "radical monotheism," a belief in one God with no room for little "gods" like the gods of country and money and material possessions. But Raines never explained anything about the nature of that one God. He never offered a specific path to reach God nor a particular doctrine to embrace.

Instead, Raines left us in a state of uncertainty and irreverence. He was an iconoclast, like Abraham. On more than one occasion, he'd end the class by breathing deeply, pulling himself together, and somberly staring at some remote, far-off place in the distance; then he would gaze at us intensely and intone that ultimately, one day, each of us would be left to stand at the edge of a dark and endless abyss of emptiness where we would have to fend for ourselves.

At that time of my life, I was already struggling with the religious observances required to be a Jew in good standing. After all, only a year earlier the cover of Time Magazine posed the question: "Is God Dead?" Holden Caulfield and Yossarian were like Jiminy Cricket perched on my shoulder when I attended the high holiday services, where admission required the purchase of a high holiday ticket and the congregants dressed to the nines, filling the seats which otherwise remained nearly empty most of the year. I would say later that the reason I stopped attending synagogue was because I developed an allergy to diamonds, minks and custom-tailored suits. In truth, I stopped because I began to read the English translation on the page opposite the Hebrew and found the words meaningless at best and objectionable at worst.

But still, it wasn't until Yossarian, Holden and Abraham-the-idol-smasher were joined by several of the Jewish prophets who had launched the "prophetic tradition" denouncing hypocrisy, introduced to me by John Raines, that I ceased attending synagogue services altogether. Which wasn't easy because my other shoulder was sagging under the onerous weight of Oma and Opa, their siblings and nieces and nephews murdered by the Nazis, and the six million annihilated in the Holocaust. Even worse, if that was possible, was the distress in my mother's voice each time she would say, "So you are not going to services?" accompanied by sorrow brimming in her brown eyes, drowning me in swells of guilt.

I could not turn my back on the Holocaust. But going to services would be hypocritical and no way to carry on the memory of the Shoah's victims. I would just have to find other means to remember them. Which is not to say I no longer wanted to be a Jew. In fact, it was just the opposite. I found something that made me proud being a Jew: to be irreverent and an iconoclast like Abraham; to be a debunker like Isaiah; to carry on the prophetic tradition; all of which was at the core of being Jewish. And none of which I learned by attending Hebrew school, or from my bar mitzvah training, or participating in and sometimes leading the youth services, or becoming confirmed after additional years of Jewish education. My pride in being a Jew grew out of what I was taught by John Raines, a pro-

The Tree of Sorrow

fessor and Methodist minister, in an introductory religion course at Temple University when I was nineteen.

Four years later, on the evening of March 8, 1971, a group of dissidents broke into the FBI office in Media, Delaware County, Pennsylvania. I learned of it in the local news media. They made off with more than a thousand files involving the government's surveillance activities on civil rights leaders and anti-war protestors. The troupe turned over their findings to the Washington Post which published the disclosures. Books were written about the event and its ramifications, and a documentary movie was made. The FBI aggressively pursued the culprits, but they were never captured nor their identities unearthed. That is, not until more than four decades had passed.

I was on vacation, having my morning coffee and reading a complimentary copy of the New York Times when I opened to a page and saw an old man peering back at me with a vaguely familiar face. The man's name leaped out from the caption. It was John Raines, and he had come forward to announce that he and his wife had been part of the gang that burglarized the Delaware County FBI headquarters in 1971. He broke his silence for a number of reasons: he had secured the permission of the surviving members of the crew; the statute of limitations had long since expired; the possibility of his children growing up with their parents in jail was no longer a consideration; he had retired from teaching duties at Temple; and it was time to come clean although, of course, he had no regrets. I read the article with great interest and resolved to contact him when I returned home since he lived a short drive from my house.

John Raines resided in the Germantown section of Philadelphia. It was a neighborhood with centuries of history including a famous Revolutionary battle—the Battle of Germantown. The main street was constructed of cobblestones, and trollies still traversed the tracks. It was adjacent to Chestnut Hill, where the houses were also of stone and brick and the community had its own prestigious history. But Chestnut Hill was populated mostly by gentry—white Protestants who traced their family trees to prior centuries, parents who sent their kids to all-white private schools where Catholics and Jews were excluded, a constituency that was a Republican bastion in an otherwise mostly Democratic city, and so on. Germantown, on the other hand, was a work in progress: whites were returning to a neighborhood previously abandoned to Blacks, with the idea to live in an integrated community where everyone could be engaged; a food cooperative was established and thriving; people joined groups that were socialist oriented and concerned about the welfare of working men and women rather than attending chicken plate fundraisers for Democratic or Republican candidates; putting an end to the Vietnam War and following that, dare it be said, to all war; and so on. And with his shirtsleeves rolled up to the elbows, deeply involved in it all, was John Raines.

For a year or so, on a corner of my desk, I kept the article with his picture in a pile of things meant to be attended to. I'd come upon it every few weeks, still determined to contact him and tell him how much of an effect he had on my beliefs and my writing, and yet, I never did. The next time I saw his picture in the paper was in an obituary article when he died on November 12, 2017, half a century from when he profoundly affected my life. Whether John Raines found himself overlooking that dark and endless abyss of emptiness or found himself standing at the foot of the gilded throne of God, I can easily visualize the twinkle in his eye and see him strutting about, waving his unlit cigar while decimating an icon or two.

Chapter Eight
The Meaning of Life: Part Two

Up until a year before I started Temple, Oma had been living with us ever since we moved to Wyncote. She had attained octogenarian status, an accomplishment for anyone at that time and even more so by someone who endured two and a half years in a concentration camp. To aid with her increasing physical frailty, my mother hired a young German woman who spoke little English but whose ability to speak German made her well suited to tend to Oma. Hilda was tall and broad shouldered; she had short, blond hair and blue eyes and rosy cheeks. In other words, an elderly Jewish survivor of the Holocaust was put in the care of a picture-perfect specimen of the Aryan race. Despite the irony, Hilda was devoted to Oma and did everything possible to make her life comfortable. Unfortunately, Hilda was powerless to defeat the onslaught of dementia that began to debilitate Oma. None of us could.

Arrangements were made for Oma to live in the Jewish Home for the Aged which was about a fifteen-minute car ride away. My mother went there every weekday, and her sister, Irma, who worked during the week, covered the weekends. The Home was off Broad Street and on my way to Temple, so once I began to matriculate at Temple, I'd stop and see Oma weekly.

The visits were pretty much one like the other. I'd park my car and enter the two-story brick building running the length of a half block. It was recently constructed, and for an "old age home" or "nursing home," as these institutions were then called, the Jewish Home was considered one of the finest. Which isn't saying much. There was no need to sign in, and I'd just smile to whoever was at the reception desk and then turn to my left and begin the trek down the hallway to Oma's room. I had to brace myself for that task which I hated.

If I could have run, I would have, but all I could do was scurry down the gauntlet of the wheelchair-lined corridor, never being fast enough to escape the haunted gazes glaring at me from the wizened faces of the residents—mostly women in loose-fitting dresses, hands lying listlessly on laps often covered with blankets, and some with their heads tilted to the side and napkins leftover from lunch still tucked into their collars. Here and there would be a bobbing head flashing a smile in the sea of scowls, and I'd quickly smile back and scuttle along. What did they want from me? Their misery was not my fault. But I felt guilty nonetheless.

Oma's room was at the end of the hall, and once I made it there, I'd breathe a sigh of relief. Stepping through the doorway, I felt as if I was back in her bedroom in Wyncote. Even in her mid-eighties, she maintained the same slim frame of her youth draped by a gray flower-patterned dress. Her hair was pulled back in a bun, and she wore her glasses at all times. Though she only needed her wheelchair for traveling out of her room, she would be sitting

The Tree of Sorrow

on it when I entered since it served the dual purpose of providing a seat for her while leaving the only chair in the room available for a guest. There was the bed, a bureau filled with her personal belongings atop which sat family photos and a nightstand. On the nightstand was a photograph of her parents, herself and eight siblings taken years before Hitler's rise to power. Several times during each visit, Oma would point to the photo and tell me that her sisters and brothers were all living in Israel. I would nod and smile, reinforcing the pretense we had created for her in the last few years from which she could take some solace. No reason to keep reminding her they were all long dead; some at the hands of the Nazis.

Sometimes, I would get behind the wheelchair, push it and take Oma on an excursion through the building. If the weather was accommodating, we'd go outside where she could enjoy the trees and shrubs, the birds and squirrels. Oma always loved gardens and small animals. At other times, we'd just sit in her room and talk; Oma mostly in German and me in my concoction of our two languages. Somehow, we'd be able to make our thoughts known to one another. It was mostly small talk but not always. And on one occasion, with the pronouncement of one word, Oma set me on a path where I would remain for the rest of my life.

This day occurred in the late spring of 1967, about half a year before she died. The semester with John Raines had concluded. I told Oma about my brother's bar mitzvah which she was unable to attend. I informed her that Frani and I just got engaged and she smiled, revealing her dentures that were loosely fitted in her mouth and not floating in the glass of water on her nightstand. She liked Frani, and Oma was a tough sell. I reminded her that I was halfway through college and that I planned on going on to law school. That was when Oma spoke the word.

"*Gerechtigkeit.*" She said I had *gerechtigkeit*. I wasn't exactly sure what the word meant, but I had an idea. Once I got home, I pulled out my German/English dictionary and looked it up. It meant justice. Oma believed I had a sense for justice. In fact, on subsequent visits, when she would ask what I planned to do and I'd say that I wanted to be a lawyer, she would tap me on the shoulder with her finger, repeat the word and say I was always like that.

For me, that meant everything. It sounded right, and it fit right. Law without justice was a travesty. I harbored no strong feelings about "the law" or practicing the law, but I was passionate about justice, or as Oma would say, *gerechtigkeit*. Nor was this passion limited to the law. Any perception I'd have of an injustice taking place in any aspect of life would incense me, and I'd find myself having to speak out and do something. I could not sit back in silence. That would be just like Oma's German neighbors spying from the slit in their window curtains while she and Opa, each lugging a suitcase, slinked from their home and into the darkness of night, never to return.

And so, that was that. In the spring of 1967, my sights were firmly set. I would be a lawyer and bring some justice to the world, my incessant search for the meaning of life notwithstanding. With that in mind, I registered for not one but two law courses in the upcoming fall semester: Administrative Law and Constitutional Law, both taught by Professor Benjamin Schoenfeld, who bore the moniker of Uncle Ben.

I'm not sure why some of the students, usually frat brothers sniggering amongst themselves, referred to Schoenfeld as Uncle Ben, but it was never to his face nor in his presence where he might overhear it. Though Schoenfeld could have been called Doctor Professor Benjamin Schoenfeld Esquire, since he held both a law degree and a PhD in political science, his physical stature was

The Tree of Sorrow

not in the least impressive. He reminded me more of a meek bookkeeper than a college professor and attorney; nor did his mien reflect his myriad of accomplishments that preceded his tenure at Temple. I never had an inkling that this mild little man who wore woolen sport jackets and trousers and who silently slid into the classroom had been a fiery activist taking considerable risks for both the labor and civil rights movements. To me, he seemed a middle-aged nebbish who started every class by opening his briefcase and removing the law book and sheets of notes over which he fiddled until the exact minute class was set to begin. At that precise moment, he'd slip the pipe out from under his mustached lip and begin to speak. But by the end of that semester and even more so in retrospect, I came to realize that Dr. Schoenfeld had one of the keenest legal minds combined with a passion for justice that I would ever encounter.

Surprisingly, it was not the two semesters of Constitutional Law that left an indelible impression upon me but rather the class on Administrative Law. This was probably because there were only six students in the class, and given the size and the pedagogy Schoenfeld preferred (one I would follow when teaching years later), we sat in a circle, engaging in didactic discussion, debate and discourse while examining and analyzing legal cases. Although it was in the Con Law classes where an enduring reverence for the First Amendment was instilled in me, it was in Schoenfeld's small circle where I learned the Socratic Method and where the critical thinking spawned by Yossarian, Holden and Abraham matured. But the best lesson came at the end of the semester when I had to take an oral final exam.

On the day of the final, each student was instructed to meet with Schoenfeld in his office at a specific time and be prepared to answer anything that was covered during the semester. I had no idea what to expect, but as I was climbing the steps to the third floor where he had his office, my anxiety was not assuaged when, on his way down, one of my classmates gazed at me as though he had just had his organs removed to save lives without anesthesia.

"How'd it go?" I asked. He tried to speak, but his lips only quivered, and he just moved on. The door to Schoenfeld's office was open, so I walked in without knocking. He was seated at his desk writing something down, probably a grade for the student who had just left. I harrumphed; he looked up, smiled slightly and spoke.

Have a seat. I sat. Meaningless pleasantries were briefly exchanged.

Just one question, Schoenfeld said.

Just one question! Is he for real? I panicked.

How do the judges on the federal courts whose cases we studied reach their decisions?

What? Was this a trick question? This can't be happening. I need a good grade. My declared major is political science. I want to go to law school. This is crazy!

Take a minute or two, he said. Schoenfeld swiveled his chair back to face the desk, dipped his pipe into a leather pouch, stuffing it with tobacco, and used his thumb to pack it down. While he waited, he inserted the pipe in his mouth and struck a match, placing the flame an inch above the pipe's bowl. He puffed a few times until satisfied it was stoked and smoking, waved the match till the flame was out, tossing it in an ashtray, and swiveled back in my direction. He took another puff, withdrew the pipe from his mouth, smiled slightly again and said: *Well?*

I have no idea what made me say what I said that day or why I said it or even where it came from, but before I could clamp my mouth shut, the words just spilled out, and though I instantly regretted it, I couldn't haul them back in.

The Tree of Sorrow

"I think judges just make a decision how they want a case to come out and then figure out a way to get there."

Schoenfeld looked at me. I could have sworn there was a twinkle in his eye that I had never seen before. Then it was gone.

"Ok," he said. "Enjoy the semester break." I wished him well and said I would see him again next semester in Con Law II. We parted.

I received a B from Schoenfeld in the Con Law I class for that fall semester. I received an A in Administrative Law. When I think of all the final exams I had through high school, college and law school, not a one has ever been as instructive as my oral exam in Administrative Law given by Dr. Benjamin Schoenfeld. I'd go on to law school at the University of Pennsylvania where the faculty had a national reputation which was well deserved. But the best law professor I ever had was an easygoing soul whose accomplishments were unpretentiously sequestered in the past and who was content to mold minds teaching political science at Temple University. Although, Schoenfeld did have a partiality for his alma mater, Harvard Law, that he made known to me a year later. Which is another story—albeit a brief one.

It was at the start of my senior year when I was in the process of making applications to law schools that I had the occasion to look up Dr. Schoenfeld. Same building, same office, same plumes of smoke wafting from the pipe that he would intermittently insert and remove from his mouth.

Of course, I'd be happy to supply letters of recommendation. Where to?

Rutgers, Temple, Villanova and Penn, I answered. All local schools.

Why not Harvard? Dr. Schoenfeld asked, leaning back in his chair while intently staring at me.

Never considered it. Penn seems enough of a stretch. But Harvard?

I can write quite a recommendation, and I'm an alumnus. Schoenfeld gloated a bit.

Well...I have to think about it. I'm married now...and there's the lease on the apartment.... I stammered, taken by surprise at the sudden disruption in my carefully laid plans.

Think about it. You should go there if you can. Dr. Schoenfeld relit his pipe and puffed. The meeting was over.

I never had to get back to Dr. Schoenfeld about Harvard Law because I didn't have any classes with him in my senior year nor did I encounter him on campus. I did think about it but only briefly. There were ample factors to keep me in the Philadelphia area: the two-year lease, Frani's pending applications for teaching jobs after graduation, our families and friends all here, my very part-time job in Dad's office, not to mention the sheer tumult of moving. But looking back on it, there had to be something more at work because how much was involved in making one more application? Likely, I wouldn't have been accepted, and even if I was, I could have made my decision at that time. Why close the door prematurely and not even try?

The answer was in one word: safe. My fear wasn't that I would be rejected. My fear was that I would get in. Then I'd have to deal with all those issues involving moving to Boston. Up to then, I had lived within a ten-mile radius all my life (and would continue to do so). I wasn't comfortable with change or the unforeseen or taking risks. I needed time to think things through, conceive a plan and not deviate. Nothing unexpected. No surprises. But why?

Dad took chances. He may not have been born with that temperament, but it certainly was fostered by what he endured in the first twenty-three years of his life:

The Tree of Sorrow

the Great Depression coupled with a father who would struggle against tuberculosis for a decade until succumbing that left the family in poverty and Dad hawking the morning and evening newspapers from the age of eight; Dad contracting TB at nineteen; meeting his future wife, also a patient in a TB sanatorium, and having her die in his arms a few years later. In other words, from the time he was a kid, Dad had nothing to lose so no reason to play it safe. And by the time he did have something to lose, risk-taking came second nature. It's part of why he was successful in business.

But I did not bask in Dad's aura. Instead, I hovered in the foreboding shadows cast by Oma, Opa and Mother, who at one time did have much to lose and indeed had lost it all. Although their lives were spared, they witnessed so many others swiftly snuffed out, leaving a permanent reminder of their own mortality. Whatever they came to possess, they clutched with hands clasped and knuckles turning crimson in an unremitting grip. With Dad, the future was a challenge filled with opportunities to secure a better life. But for my mother and her family, they once had that better life, and it was cruelly stolen; for them, the future was something to be feared and was fraught with danger and loss. My mother and her parents were entrenched in the soil of safety, and it was in that same terra firma where I germinated and grew and, like them, was destined to remain.

The following year—my last at Temple—I took a course entitled Jewish Existentialism, with Maurice Friedman who had been my professor in Modern Jewish Religious Thought two years earlier and had arranged for us to hear Elie Wiesel. While I found the course on Jewish existentialism to be intellectually stimulating, ironically, it was the earlier course with Friedman that affected me deeply in an existential way.

Richard D. Bank

On that first day of class about modern Jewish thought, twenty or so students filled the seats when Professor Friedman entered. He was a middle-aged, round man with a fleshy face, dressed in slacks and a sport jacket, white shirt and tie. But what struck me immediately was that he was wearing a beret, which he took off after he seated himself. Appearing a bit exhausted from his walk to class, he wiped some sweat from his forehead, took a deep breath, and asked everyone to form a circle with their chairs. The screeches from the metal legs of the chairs and the grousing of the students trying to arrange themselves in a circumference stretching around the entire room created a cacophony grating on the patience of everyone—except the man who sat with the calf of one leg resting on the knee of the other leg, calmly observing the muddle he had created. As the semester wore on, we would become more and more proficient in arranging the circle before each class and at the conclusion restoring the chairs to their prior positions in orderly rows.

But make no mistake, the circle was an essential element of Friedman's philosophy predicated on the teachings of Martin Buber. This meant relating to the world and everything and everybody in it by way of "Dialogue." Thus, from a pedagogical point of view, the only way to conduct a course was in a circle. Introducing me to the works of Martin Buber, most notably *I and Thou*, would have a lasting and profound effect upon how I would think and how I would live the rest of my life.

Nevertheless, the most consequential thing to ever happen to me during my four-year sojourn on Temple's campus occurred on a bright, sunny day with the leaves of the trees bursting in full fall foliage, infusing the view from our classroom as Professor Friedman entered and instructed us to return our chairs to orderly rows. With

The Tree of Sorrow

puzzled looks, furrowed foreheads and muffled grumbling, we complied.

Follow me please, he said, striding through the doorway and heading down the hall at the end of which he entered an empty classroom. The room was dark while we took our seats but became black as a moonless night when Professor Friedman drew down the shades and then flipped the last light switch off. It was then I noticed a light beaming from a movie projector, shining onto a screen at the front of the room. Friedman settled into the chair by the projector, catching his breath and removing his beret while wiping the sweat from his brow.

This is a French documentary with subtitles, Professor Friedman explained. *It runs about the length of our class time so when it's over, you are free to leave*, he added without a smile. It was a Friday, and this was my last class of the day. What a great way to begin the weekend, I thought to myself as Friedman flicked the switch and the movie began.

I have long ago forgotten the narrative of that film, if I fully absorbed it in the first place. I only recall fragments and what followed after the movie ended, when the screen turned white under the blare of a filmless projector still running.

I remember barbed wire fences against which faces were pressed, almost all appearing eerily identical: thin, beak-like nostrils, scrawny chins squeezing through the square openings of the fence, desperately seeking escape, hairless heads, ghostly eyes opened wide with nary a blink. Only on the front row could bodies be discerned clad in striped outfits looking like pajamas hanging limply on the skeletal figures and behind that, rows and rows of faces peering bleakly with just a hint of curiosity directed at whoever was holding the camera.

There was a man-made mountain, or so I thought. My mind was unable to comprehend the composition of the mound, having never been presented with anything like it before. But the camera remained steady and fixed on the mountain, allowing time for me to finally grasp what my eyes were seeing. The hill was neither stone nor dirt nor rocks nor rubbish. It was a heap of flesh and bones and follicles of pubic hair. Scraggly arms were flung and thrusted like twisted and bent branches from a dying tree. Gaunt heads hung from limp and broken necks. Legs were misshapen and stretched, unable to flee from the mass of naked torsos that comprised that dune of death.

There were deep ditches with more bare bodies heaped one atop the other. There were shabbily suited soldiers, obviously prisoners: some seated upon soil; some meandering the perimeter of a fenced-in area; some standing stiffly against a wall as one by one, they slumped to the ground after being shot. There were other soldiers in worn but presentable uniforms, all looking grim as they absorbed the surroundings they had just inherited. There was a sign reading, "*Arbeit Macht Frei*," which from the German I knew meant something like, "work makes freedom."

While the film ran its course, nothing was said in the room—not even muffled words. There were sporadic noises, however: gasps, groans, sniffles, whimpers, whispers. At the end when whiteness returned to the screen and the film's final frames flapped freely in the air, Professor Friedman turned the projector off and switched the lights back on. He looked at us and nodded, meaning we could leave. The chairs screeched but more softly than usual. We gathered our things and belongings and one by one made our way through the room and to the door exiting into the hallway. Not a word was spoken; the silence was deafening. No eye contact was made. Feet shuffled down

The Tree of Sorrow

the corridor and the stairway leading to the bright sunshine outside and the smack of fresh air.

I made my way to the parking lot and my car. As I exited the lot and navigated the narrow streets with the sidewalks teeming with students hustling home for the weekend, I turned onto Broad Street which I could mindlessly traverse for the next five miles. I put the radio on but within seconds, I turned it off. I don't remember what I was thinking, and indeed, I'm not sure I was thinking anything. It was as if I was in a trance and my mind was as blank as the movie screen when the film came to an end. About halfway down Broad Street, as I passed the building where Oma was then living in the nursing unit, I felt tears streaming down my cheeks. I heard someone bawling like a wild animal, but I was alone in the car. Where were the cries coming from? Surely not from me?

I was drowning in a lethal mixture of anguish and anger. Coursing through my veins was an aimless surge of determination to do something—anything—but I didn't know what. For the first time in my life, I had come face to face with the Holocaust.

In the weeks that followed and as the tree branches transmogrified from the browns and oranges and yellows of their shriveling leaves to bare limbs that twisted and turned under the brunt of winter's wind, I immersed myself into the world of Europe a quarter of a century earlier and what it was like to be a Jew at that place and time. I read Elie Wiesel's *Night* that was assigned in class as a precursor to hearing him speak, and on my own, I read *Treblinka*, which was about one of the more infamous concentration camps and was one of the few brutally honest books about the Holocaust then available. I'd read them at night before shutting off the light and trying to sleep since I never knew which page would trigger tears welling in my eyes. I wanted to know as much as I could about the

Holocaust, but I knew not to ask Mother, who would only respond with stoic silence, nor Oma, who was failing and confined mostly to her bed at the nursing home where in a few months, I would see her for the last time with an oxygen tent shrouding her lifeless body.

Struggling with the Holocaust encompassing the murder of six million Jews, I had determined that the topic for my term paper in Professor Friedman's class would be, "Can God Withstand the History of the Jewish People?" which covered the two millennia of persecution they endured in the Diaspora, culminating in the Holocaust. How could an omnipotent God allow such a thing? Or perhaps God is not so omnipotent after all? But if that's true, then how could God be "God"? I examined some of the arguments scholars and theologians had put forth including one suggesting that it was the price paid for the establishment of the state of Israel. In the end, I found them all to be deficient.

My ultimate response to the question I posed in my paper was existential and occurred one night after re-visiting a chapter in *Treblinka*. Filled with despair, I placed the hefty book about Treblinka on my nightstand and picked up the lightweight paperback copy of Buber's *I and Thou*, written in expressive prose. Despite the book's brevity and cogent style, the message was profound: God is not anthropomorphic like an old bearded man in the sky; rather, God is the Eternal Thou and ephemeral, encountered in the "between" of a genuine 'I and Thou" Dialogue that only occurs when one opens oneself up completely to the "Otherness" of the other (a person, animal, inanimate object—anything). One comes away from that experience not with any specific knowledge to speak of—words are inadequate. But one does come away with a certainty that the occurrence did indeed take place. Sometimes, that experience includes "meeting" the Eternal Thou, or "God,"

The Tree of Sorrow

but this is the exception and not the rule. Employing a metaphor, Buber speaks of the "Thou" encounter to be like a fleeting butterfly ensconced by an eternal chrysalis consisting of everyday life, or the world of "I-It." Yet, one must always be open to take advantage of the encounter whenever the opportunity presents itself.

As Buber's words melded with the world of *Treblinka*, I felt myself inexplicably drawn into the encounter. I experienced a Presence and felt a confirmation that God did in fact withstand the history of the Jewish People including the Holocaust, but I was unable to put this into words. Such was my conclusion in the paper that I submitted at semester's end.

I received a B++ for the paper from Professor Friedman. He thought it to be a very fine work that could have more scholarly research added. I was disappointed to an extent. Not so much with the grade. Rather, that Professor Friedman, the acknowledged authority on Martin Buber, had seemed to have missed the point I was trying to make which was: there is no "answer" to the question posed by the title of my paper; at most, only an unspoken affirmation for which words must fail.

My final semester at Temple was in the spring of 1969—a tumultuous time in America. President Nixon was merely months into his first term, and it was already clear that despite his campaign promise to bring an end to the Vietnam conflict with his "secret plan," which he had touted throughout the campaign, he was in no haste to do so. Body bags returning the remains of soldiers killed each week were counted by the hundreds, and it was little solace that the reported "kills" of the enemy were in the thousands while the war ravaged on. Protests—sometimes confrontational and even violent—flared across the country's campuses. But not so much at Temple with its proletarian population where students were focused on earning a degree and securing a pathway to coveted careers; although this peacefulness would detonate soon after I graduated.

It was in this fractious state of affairs that I enrolled in a new course offered by the political science department entitled American Political Theory, taught by Dr. Peter Bachrach who had been lured from Bryn Mawr College, a small, elite liberal arts school for women outside Philadelphia. His reputation as a giant in his field—respected, published and popular—had preceded him. When I entered the classroom for the first class, I was barely able to snare a seat before they filled entirely, leaving several students standing. The professor was already seated behind a desk at the front of the room. Although not tardy, I never arrived before he did nor would I observe him leave after the end of class. During class, he remained in his chair behind the desk, though I vaguely recall seeing him once or twice perambulating about campus with the aid of crutches. No one ever spoke of his disability, which I surmised might have been the result of polio given that his generation was the last to bear the brunt of the disease before the vaccines were available. But neither this nor his slight physique diminish what became clear by the end of the semester—he was a man passionate about democracy and preserving its values and institutions.

We read works about politics and government in the United States by some of the Founding Fathers, and others by the likes of de Tocqueville, Veblen and Dewey. Yet the one that intrigued me the most was a brief book listed on the syllabus as optional reading entitled, *The Theory of Democratic Elitism*, by Peter Bachrach, in which he argued that democracy cannot persist without the support of "the common man." I was always fully engaged in class discussions and still remember how Dr. Bachrach ended one of the more spirited exchanges.

The Tree of Sorrow

I can't recall the specifics of the topic at hand, but his final observation proved prescient. Looking around the room wearing his customary affable expression, he cautioned us not to become complacent that the calls for civil rights and the demands to end the war in Vietnam and bring honesty and accountability to government were faits accomplis. Growing somber, he stared at some distant spot over and above our heads, saying that in ten or twenty years most of us will likely be out on golf courses negotiating business deals and the dreams we now have will be recalled as a naïve stage in our lives. He didn't say this with disparagement. Rather, his voice was filled with resignation, even sadness. At the time, I don't think any of us gave his prediction much credence, but as the years have passed, I believe it proved true for most of my generation.

By the time the semester was over, I embraced Bachrach's view that the ruling establishment cannot be allowed to ride roughshod over the individual and that the individual is paramount. While this became a keystone in my belief system, what left an even more indelible mark upon me occurred after the course's last class.

About ten minutes before the end of that class, Dr. Bachrach placed a pile of blue books on his desk and announced he'd be returning our final exams. The exam had consisted of two essay questions with one being labeled as "more important" and asking whether we considered ourselves to be free or not and what we could do to expand our freedom. Just before he began calling us up to retrieve our exams, he said something about one of the students earning an A+ and that this was only the second time in his teaching career he ever awarded that grade. When I heard my name, I walked up to his desk, took the blue book from his extended hand and returned his smile. After taking my seat, I quickly flipped the pages to the last one and saw an A+.

In the late 60s, along with questioning just about everything, utilizing letter grades to reflect a student's work came under scrutiny as presenting an obstacle to the pursuit of knowledge. Even at Temple, by my senior year, we had an option to elect a Pass/Fail grade for one course. When I arrived at Penn Law that fall, letter grades had been dispensed with in their entirety and replaced with words: Distinguished, Excellent, Good, Qualified and Unsatisfactory, which really was just window dressing for the letters they supplanted. Hence, while the A+ meant little in and of itself, coming from Peter Bachrach, I couldn't help but being elated and felt I had to say something to him.

When the class was dismissed, I slowly made my way to the front of the room where several students were gathered around his desk expressing whatever parting words and questions they had on their minds. I held back, watching Dr. Bachrach engage them in his easy-going manner. One by one, the students peeled off, and finally, I was left standing alone, shifting back and forth awkwardly with nothing specific to say. But we did converse for a moment or two, though I remember nothing of it other than something he did and something he called me.

The thing that he did was give me the name and phone number of an attorney who provided pro bono work for the ACLU. He said I should contact her and reference his name when I started law school in the fall to see if I could assist her. In fact, I would do just that, and I did research on two cases which began a lifetime involvement with the ACLU.

The second thing I remember was the words he spoke to me as we made our good-byes. I turned and started to walk out of the room when Dr. Bachrach called after me, exclaiming that one day I might just find myself being the world's "last humanist." I stopped, turned and smiled, somewhat unsure what he meant by that. He smiled back broadly and that was the last time I ever saw him. But as the years have passed, I have never forgotten what he said and am still honored that he said it.

Chapter Nine
An Outsider Again

When I was thirteen, the movie *Exodus* was released. I had already read the historical novel by Leon Uris about the birth of the modern Jewish state so there was little for me to learn from the movie, but I didn't expect to be disappointed, which I was. I knew nothing of the difficulties of transferring a monumental work like *Exodus* to the screen and the need for massive editing that removed the entire narrative of the pre-partitioned years and the wrenching backstory that took place in the Warsaw ghetto. But when I took my seat in the ornate movie theater in Center City, Philadelphia along with my dad and a friend of mine, I was still expecting something momentous to happen once the baroque curtains were drawn. Two seats were empty on the other side of Dad that he was holding for his mother and the man he called Mr. Lyons.

Dad kept craning his neck, looking back and scanning the crowd making its way down the aisle in search of his mother, whom I called Bobbie. It was a snowy day, and

The Tree of Sorrow

the drive into the city was difficult. Bobbie and Mr. Lyons (whom I called *Zayde* Lyons) lived in West Philadelphia, and Bobbie would not hear of Dad going so far out of his way—in a snowstorm no less—to pick them up when all they had to do was walk one block and take a bus directly to the movie theater. My dad could be stubborn, but he was never a match for the obstinance and determination in the steely blue eyes of his mother whom he worshipped. The look of relief on his face when he spotted them at the top of the aisle transformed into a smile as he leaped from his seat to retrieve them.

For Bobbie, watching *Exodus* was a dream come true. That would be the closest she'd get to being in Israel. She would often talk to me about Israel, sometimes saying, "Richard, I would kiss the ground of our homeland if I ever get there," and her roundish face would beam. Indeed, for whatever reason, despite a most difficult life, Bobbie was often beaming and never more so than during that three-and-a-half-hour movie. Hearing the theme song, which I had just learned to play on the trumpet, watching Jews battle for the right to live in freedom in the biblical land that once had been theirs, seeing a safe harbor that had been foreclosed to so many European Jews, including my grandparents, and feeling a warmth inside my chest every time I glanced over and saw Bobbie glowing, all made me determined to get myself to Israel. Which I did, along with Frani, in the summer of 1969—a graduation present from Mother and Dad.

On July 20, 1969, Neil Armstrong was the first man to step on the moon. Hundreds of millions of pairs of eyes around the globe were glued to TV sets, awestruck by that milestone in human history. But not me nor my not-so-happy spouse as we exited the tour bus with our group for a midnight excursion to the Wailing Wall, the last standing vestige of the Holy Temple in Jerusalem, reclaimed two years earlier in the Six Day War. I didn't mind missing the fuzzy camera shots of Armstrong's booted feet silently clunking on the lunar surface nor hearing his memorable words about a step for man and a leap for mankind or whatever. At the time, I believed humanity was better served by utilizing the billions spent on a race to the moon for something else like feeding the hungry. Frani, on the other hand, harbored no such qualms and was more than miffed to have missed this singular historic event, instead forced to have her shoulders sheathed with a shawl to maintain feminine modesty and keep a proper distance from a stony wall women were not allowed to approach.

But going to the Wailing Wall, seeing the ancient sites, spending a night in a kibbutz, even meeting some of Mother's cousins was not the highlight of the twelve-day trip. For me, the focus was on Israel's memorial to the victims of the Holocaust, *Yad Vashem*. When I visited in '69, the facility had only been open for twelve years; decades later, it would be expanded to a complex four times the original size and be a prominent fixture on Mount Herzl, the Mount of Remembrance.

When we arrived at *Yad Vashem*, the normally loquacious group we travelled with took on a solemn demeanor. Even the Hadassah women who were always pointing here and there, opining on what they saw and *kvelling* about every site shown—especially the Hadassah Hospital we visited—were subdued. Now these gray-haired ladies kept their arms stiffly at their sides, their rouge lips tight and their eyes looking vacant as we followed our Israeli-born guide until he delivered us to the docent who would lead us through the corridors of the Holocaust memorial.

There is much I do not remember of what we were shown, but I do remember a pile of shoes—hundreds and hundreds of pairs, shoes of all sorts and colors having one

The Tree of Sorrow

thing in common; they were small. They were the shoes of murdered children. I recall numerous photographs of victims posted along the walls we passed: old and young; male and female; big and little; light haired and swarthy haired; blue eyed, brown eyed, hazel eyed, green eyed; some Russian, some German, some Polish, some French, some Greek; some of everything. Some men wore beards and skullcaps and *payess*; other men were clean-shaven, hatless and decked out in three-piece suits with stiff collars and starched shirts; some women wore stylish frocks; other women wore *shmattes*. But they all had one thing in common. They were all killed because they were Jews.

A final stop, we were informed, and then we could browse before boarding our bus. One by one, we exited a well-lit corridor and entered a vast vaulted room barely illuminated by what seemed to be countless flickering candles or night-lights. Making some introductory remarks, the docent pointed to the massive surface before us where bronze plaques each bore the name of a concentration camp. After he finished, he gazed out at the barren space and somberly nodded. Silence suffused the chamber. Just a few minutes to absorb what lie at my feet.

Which one is Theresienstadt? I needed to know. Auschwitz. Treblinka. Sobibor. Dachau. My eyes scanned all those near me. I paced in one direction and then another. But no Theresienstadt. It had to be here. I asked the guide. *Yes, it must be here*, he said. But he did not know where. Once again, I was starkly reminded that in the history of the Holocaust, Theresienstadt was merely an inconsequential footnote thus reinforcing the notion that my grandparents didn't have it so bad after all and leaving me as their apologist. It would be decades later that I would learn how wrong I was accepting the Nazi fabrication, as did most of the world, that Theresienstadt was a "paradise ghetto," when in fact, it was anything but.

I began to panic knowing that I had to find the plaque before the time elapsed to board the bus. I scurried along one side wall and then darted back to the other side. Finally, in a remote corner, I saw it. Theresienstadt. It was like a grave marker covering the memory of Oma and Opa. Their bodies are buried in the earth outside Philadelphia. Their years lived in Theresienstadt lie here.

My hand gripped the Kodak Instamatic I was holding. I pulled myself out from the surreal state I was in and snapped a photo. *Time to leave*, I heard the docent say. I turned and saw Frani waving me toward the door. I returned and followed everyone into the blaring summer sun set high above Mount Herzl. I left something behind on the plaque bearing the word Theresienstadt, and I took something with me when I left.

Jenkintown, Pennsylvania is a tiny borough adjacent to Cheltenham Township, where I lived my teenage years. It's divided in half by a major road with numerous commercial establishments on either side. Narrow streets crisscross the area, necessitating many to be designated as "one-way," meaning if you make the wrong turn you can find yourself trapped like a mouse in a maze unable to get back on track. Beyond the commercial district, single-family homes of various sizes and shapes, most built of stone or brick and constructed pre-WWII, line the constricted streets. Sitting unobtrusively amongst those dwellings is a white stucco ranch house, barely 1,000 square feet, that, unlike its neighbors, was not occupied by a family. To most of the general public, what went on inside was a mystery.

Other than bronze numerals affixed to the front door denoting the address, there was nothing to identify the structure. No name, no signage, no advertisement for a business, no nothing. On weekday mornings, several people would arrive, and during the day, others, mostly

The Tree of Sorrow

young men, sporadically would go in and out within a brief span of time. Beige shades were always drawn on all the windows so the goings-on inside were not visible. By five o'clock each weekday, the building was vacated, except for several nights during each month when a handful of cars were parked outside and lights illuminated the shades so that shadows could be discerned. The anonymity of the place was purposefully designed for the protection of those within. The first time I entered the building was in the summer of 1965, soon after I had turned eighteen when I was required to register with the Selective Service.

    I remember very little of that day since it was more a formality than a momentous occasion to sign up for the draft. In a way, it was a coming-of-age sort of thing. The draft board's office looked innocuous enough. File cabinets backed up against the walls allowing scant space for the several desks piled high with papers, forms and folders. A bored-looking white-haired woman waved me over to her desk where I received a form, filled it out, signed my name and returned it, giving little concern that I had just been added to a list of men who might be sent to a far off place to kill and be killed. Vietnam was little more than a remote nuisance at the time though that would soon change.

    Just weeks later, I received my draft card in the mail with the classification of 1A which meant I was among those available to be summoned for service. I was unperturbed, however, because I knew that in September, my status would convert to 2S which provided a student deferment for the entire four years I would be an undergrad so long as I maintained the requisite GPA. The problem was that except for medical and dental school, all graduate programs, including law, would no longer be eligible for student deferment. At eighteen, four years seemed a long way off to be worried about that, and so I wasn't.

But things moved fast. The Vietnam conflict developed a voracious appetite for young men with 1A status, gobbling them up and spewing out the remains into body bags. I wasn't particularly patriotic and needed a good reason to fight for my country. Vietnam did not provide that reason, and I wasn't inclined to delay my plans for law school or lay my life on the line for what was seeming to me to be an immoral war. There must be options to avoid this somehow. There had to be. Contingency plans must be made!

I could become a farmer. They were exempt from the draft. Dad said he would buy me a farm in New Jersey, and I could go to law school as well. But what did I know of farming? I didn't like animals, hated vegetables and suffered from seasonal allergies when outside.

Perhaps I could join the Pennsylvania National Guard. In those days, the national guard meant just that. Its mission was to defend the country, not go overseas to war. But there was no room; even the waiting list was closed. Obviously, I wasn't the only one panicking. Not only was the Guard filled, but so was the medic corps in the Air Force where my older cousin served in the reserves. Joining the reserves wasn't a bad idea; it entailed a six-month period of active duty and then seven years of one weekend a month and two weeks in the summer. And being a medic sounded safe, even a principled thing to do. I'd be saving people, not killing them. And I could still go to law school—just a year delay. But all the medic units were full, and I would have been terrible at it anyway. I barely passed high school biology, and I still remember my teacher grimacing as he examined the frog I had finished dissecting and muttering something about the toad looking like it had been put through a blender.

The Tree of Sorrow

I could apply for conscientious objector status, but that required proclaiming I was opposed to all war on religious grounds based upon a belief in God. But I wasn't opposed to all wars. Certainly not WWII and the Israeli War of Independence. And my opposition to Vietnam had nothing to do with God and religion. It was a moral stance. It was simply wrong.

Then there was the old adage: make a run for it. Run and hide until it was over. But I knew Frani wouldn't want to leave her family and do that, so Canada was likely out, though I held on to it as a remote possibility.

A more feasible alternative would be to take a teaching position after graduating college. Teachers were exempt from the draft, and I could go to law school at night. Male teachers were in demand—especially in Philadelphia. Of course, my degree was not in education, but I could teach gym or possibly get a job in a private school. Problem was that I was a poor physical specimen carrying thirty pounds I could do without. While I lifted weights sporadically, I had hated gym class in all its aspects: petrified of climbing the rope, terrified at the thought of thrusting myself over the "horse," almost always the last in the pack to "run" the 100 yard dash, never played a sport after the age of thirteen and had no desire to ever do so. Nonetheless, this seemed my best option, and that was my plan until the summer of '68. I had one year left on my 2S status when Dad informed me he had made a contact. A very good one.

It seemed that on those several nights a month when the blinds were drawn especially tight and shadowy figures could be discerned from inside the Selective Service's stucco building, a handful of men were meeting to determine what names to cull from the "available" list to match the number needed for their monthly quota to replenish the military ranks. The men who made this determination comprised the local Selective Service Board. They had no specific qualifications, and their appointments were purely political, as was the chairman's. These men remained nameless to the public, but from a business associate, Dad had learned the identity of the chairman, who was supposedly "well-disposed" to those opposing the war. Indeed, he was especially "sympathetic" to those distraught young men whose fathers dabbled in the stock market, utilizing his services as a stockbroker. None of which is to say that anything illegal occurred, never a specific quid pro quo, and in fact, I later learned that the chairman never interfered with the proper process in any way though he certainly did nothing to dispel the myth that he could.

The plan was simple. The chairman said that after my graduation in the spring of 1969, I would be classified 1A, and following that, I'd be called for a physical. The goal would be to obtain a 4F classification which would make me exempt from the draft due to health issues. To prepare for this, I should see my family physician, which I did. Upon a thorough examination, other than one slightly flat foot (two flat feet were necessary for the exemption), the only possible malady I presented was that I had allergies. But did my allergies cause asthma, because that's what I needed to be considered for a 4F. Dr. B., our family physician who had treated my dad when he was at a sanatorium for tuberculosis several decades earlier and who remained a good friend and the family doctor, didn't ask me whether I was wheezing but simply provided scripts for an inhaler and pills to be refilled periodically to establish a medical record.

Dr. B. also referred me to an allergist for testing. Once a week for ten weeks, a petite, gray-haired lady in a white nurse's uniform had me roll up my sleeves, and she'd stick me a dozen times on each arm with something or other ranging from pollen to cat hair to peanuts to just about

The Tree of Sorrow

anything anybody could be allergic to. After she was finished, she'd smile and leave the room, saying the doctor would be with me shortly. In about half an hour, the doctor would enter, nod, look over his spectacles at both my arms, make some notes after seeing nothing almost all of the time, smile and say he'd see me the following week.

To my dismay, other than several specks of redness, there were no changes to my arms during the entire process. But a few spots was all it took for the doctor to provide a written report to Dr. B. diagnosing me as being allergic to dust and mold spores. The doctor suggested that I'd be given a regimen of injections over a couple of months to try and desensitize me to the allergies. Dr. B. authorized that the serum be prepared but that it be sent to him to administer the injections.

By early spring before my graduation, I was making weekly visits to Dr. B. to receive the shots. Every week he'd put a stethoscope to my chest and check my blood pressure. That first week, he frowned and said my blood pressure was high for someone my age, and he counseled less red meat, more exercise and lose weight, all of which I did. He'd always ask how I was doing and continued to monitor my pressure which did improve. But he never gave me the injections for my allergies. After the number of visits reached the number of injections I was to have received, Dr. B. provided me with a two-page letter to deliver at the time of my physical for the draft. After reading it, I thought I was a dead man. I couldn't imagine any army would want someone as sickly as the person in Dr. B.'s letter.

Shortly after graduation, as prognosticated by the chairman, I received my new draft status: 1A. The armed forces needed bodies; even the Marines were drafting for the first time in their storied history. Anyone unfortunate enough to be stuck with a 1A classification was raw meat to placate the War's ravenous craving. A couple of weeks later, I received an order to report at 7:00 a.m. to the white stucco building in Jenkintown. Despite Dad receiving assurances from the chairman that everything was going smoothly and there was nothing to be concerned about, I could feel my blood pressure surge.

I was never an early riser and was bleary-eyed, pale, and more than anxious as I entered the Selective Service's office after parking my car. There were already a dozen young men in the waiting area who all looked like they would rather be somewhere else. Soon the group doubled in size, and we were told to board the yellow school bus outside. The bus door opened, and a man in a military uniform stepped off. He read names from a clipboard, and when he reached mine, like the others, I said, "Present." When he finished, he told us that for the day we were under the jurisdiction of the United States Army and to follow all instructions.

Our destination was a building on Broad Street between Temple's campus and City Hall. As I was gazing out the window, I spotted the inert body of a man sprawled on the street by the curb; his limbs were twisted, and the torso was spurting fresh blood in all directions. Several people were huddled around him, and I could see the flashing lights of an ambulance not far off. Was this some sort of an omen? My intestines went into spasms.

When we arrived, we alighted from the bus and were escorted into the building where another uniformed man took over. I recall very little of the next four or five hours that I was in that facility. But I vividly remember that after filling out forms and listening to instructions, I found myself in a locker room with about fifty other guys being ordered to remove our clothing and leave them in a locker, taking only the key attached to a wristband. My heart dropped, and I felt like I did in those recurring dreams

The Tree of Sorrow

of being given a test that I never studied for or having forgotten to do the homework assignment or being in a crowd of people and realizing I had no clothes on.

Fortunately, unlike the dream, I wasn't entirely naked since we could keep on our underpants and undershirts. But what about the plan? What about the dust I had so carefully gathered in a tissue and placed into my pants pocket so I could inhale it just before getting my physical exam and then have an asthma attack? And the inhalant I had beside it that I would retrieve to save me, proving my very life was dependent upon a prescription medication? And what about the letter from Dr. B. that was inside my other pocket? How was I supposed to give it to the doctor to read when I was examined? How was I to do any of that? What would become of the chairman's plan?

With our military escort standing arms folded by the door, sneering as everyone undressed, I furtively transferred the dust from the tissue to my left hand and with my right hand, took the letter from my trousers and held on to it for dear life. I cursed under my breath as I spilled some dust fumbling to get the locker closed. Some more spilt dust and grumbled expletives as I slipped the key band onto my wrist and joined the line heading out the door to the urinals.

"Take a cup from the shelf, piss in it halfway, hand it in as you leave and give your name," the soldier barked, strutting about. For the first time, I noticed his buzzed head, jutted jaw, meticulous uniform and that he didn't just walk but swaggered. I squeezed myself between two guys and reached to take a cup when my dilemma hit me. I needed one free hand to guide my penis. Left hand or right? I couldn't afford to lose more dust, but I must have the letter. Reluctantly, I unclenched my fist and forlornly watched as the remaining dust was swallowed by the mixture of piss and water flowing in the latrine. Given the lost dust, all the guys urinating around me, repeated shouts from Gomer Pyle to get the pissing over with, I just couldn't get started. By the time I did and finally finished, I was the last to leave.

How much time had passed and what mundane procedures we went through, I do not recollect, but eventually, I found myself seated in a large room with about thirty other guys and still fervently clutching Dr. B.'s letter. At the front of the room were three cubicles, each with a desk and one chair on either side. In each cubby, there was a young man clad in underwear sitting on a chair and seated on the other was an older man with a stethoscope hanging from his neck who was frequently looking down and writing on a sheet of paper. Every five or ten minutes, a rotation would take place in each of the cubicles, where the guy in his underwear would get up and leave, the doctor would set the piece of paper on top of a growing pile of papers, nod at Gomer Pyle, and then Gomer Pyle would snarl the name of someone who would jump from his seat and walk over to the vacated chair in the available cubicle. Clearly, this was a fair and random procedure in terms of who would be seen by which doctor. I clenched my teeth and squeezed my lips tight so my scream wouldn't escape.

This was not the chairman's plan! I was supposed to see the doctor who was supportive of the anti-war movement and didn't want lives filled with promise to be terminated in a senseless conflagration. The physician who was going to assign me a 4F based on Dr. B.'s letter and a perfunctory examination and because the chairman told him wonderful things about me. Now, I only had a one in three shot in seeing this guy. All sorts of questions were racing through my mind with answers arriving at the same conclusion. The chairman was running a scam! That was my last thought when I heard my name called.

The Tree of Sorrow

What went on in that cubicle is mostly a blur, as my mind was preoccupied with visions of the bloody body lying on Broad Street and fearing that it was a sign portending what awaited me in Vietnam. What I do remember is the doctor being a middle-aged man with a nice smile whose eyebrows arched as he read the letter I handed him and that he asked me some questions and put the stethoscope to my chest while I drew deep breaths. But that's all I recall up until when he wrote something on the paper where he had written my name and other stuff, placed it on the top of the pile, said good-bye and waved me off.

The final destination was another large room where we were to wait until summoned to the front and handed a slip of paper with our classification, and then sent on our way. After what seemed like an interminable period, I heard a uniformed minion shout my name. I scurried to the desk, struggling to control the heaving of my chest. I extended my shaking hand to receive the folded piece of paper, and I fought to restrain myself from looking at it until out the door. Once in the hallway, I unfolded the paper to learn where my life was headed—1A or 4F—law school or Nam?

What the fuck is 1Y! Had I lost my vision? I lifted the paper up to my eyes to make sure the Y was not an A. It wasn't. What does this mean? Below my name and classification, there was a list with brief explanations of the classifications. The description for 1Y said something about having a limited but not disabling health condition and being called for active duty only in case of war or national emergency. Sounded like I escaped Hell but was denied access to Heaven and sentenced to Purgatory.

After some anxious hours, Dad reached the chairman who assured him that everything was fine and went according to plan. Men with 1Y were only considered after the pool for 1A was depleted and that would probably mean something like WWIII was going on. Indeed, it was such an enigmatic classification that it was actually abolished in December 1971, and I was reclassified to 1A. But by then, the draft was based on lottery numbers utilizing birthdays. My number was 272 of 366, and the number reached in that year was well under 200. Moreover, Nixon was on his way to achieving the goal of an honorable withdrawal from Vietnam which turned out to be a helicopter whisking away desperate Americans from the roof of the United States embassy while an enraged crowd below was storming the building. For this, so many lives were wasted.

A month following my physical for the draft, in the beginning of September 1969, I started law school. I had decided not to take the train but to drive to the campus of the University of Pennsylvania located in West Philadelphia. Penn's campus was just a couple of miles from our former home on 33rd Street, and I could not help but think of this as I weaved through early morning traffic. Here I was—a product of two middle-class neighborhoods comprised mostly of Jewish families where many of the *bubbehs* and *zaydes* were European immigrants; the first in my family to graduate college; and now beginning law school dressed to the nines. I had discerned the proper attire for aspiring attorneys while at Temple where I frequently passed its law school during class breaks. The students, almost all men, wore ties and jackets as they gathered on the steps of the brownstone building to catch a smoke. So, I knew what to wear, and on that first day, I was decked out in a new blue suit, pale-blue shirt and tie and of course, carrying a briefcase. I stopped to gaze when I reached the foot of the two-hundred-year-old building that housed the law school.

Taking a deep breath, I mounted the concrete steps leading up to two massive oak doors. Penn was consid-

The Tree of Sorrow

ered an Ivy, so I wasn't surprised to see the gray stone structure actually covered with ivy. Inside, I walked under an archway and tentatively treaded on the marble floor. I found myself in a magnificent vaulted room with sunlight striking through stained glass at the dome's top. Straight ahead was a winding staircase rising several stories, which I climbed with care as I made my way into the labyrinth of both the building and the law.

The first day was an orientation session where all first-year law students were gathered in one of the two lecture halls where we would be taking the required first-year courses. By the end of the week, our class would be divided into two sections of about 100 students each. Penn was a small law school and had maintained the same class size for many years even in the face of growing applications, which allowed it to be very selective. The vast majority of the students were from outside the Philadelphia area and lived off campus in the surrounding neighborhood or in the new dormitory. Given their proximity to the school, they had already filled the room, leaving only backrow seats available by the time I arrived after my fifty-minute commute. Settling in, I cautiously surveyed my surroundings.

To my surprise, there were about twenty women, several of whom were African American, much more than the proportion of women at Temple's law school. The men were mostly my age and easily engaged in conversations with others like themselves. Several wore suits and ties; maybe a dozen wore sport jackets, but the rest were in shirts and trousers or jeans. Many had hair spilling down to the bases of their necks and thick sideburns as well as boasting facial hair—mustaches, beards and goatees. I could feel my face burning red as I imagined how out of place I must have looked with hair closely cropped, suit and tie, and briefcase in tow.

Suddenly, everyone grew quiet as a gentleman with silver hair and dressed in a three-piece pin-striped suit stepped up to the rostrum. He introduced himself as the dean and in a solemn, dignified tone, welcomed us to Penn Law. We were soon given a booklet containing our names accompanied by brief information on each of us. If I were at Temple or Villanova, I wouldn't have needed such data since almost everyone would have lived in the tri-state region and graduated from one of a handful of local colleges and universities. It's also likely I would have known more than a few, some even quite well. But as I kept searching for familiar faces in the amphitheater, I found only two I vaguely knew from high school. Where did all these people come from and who were they? So, I perused the list.

There were only four other Temple grads and even fewer from Penn State with a smidgen from other public universities. The bulk of the class hailed from the Ivy's elite eight: Yale, Harvard, Princeton, Columbia, Dartmouth, Cornell, Brown and Penn, plus Stanford, then called the Harvard of the West Coast. Several of the females in the class held degrees from the Ivies, and the rest graduated from the prestigious liberal arts women colleges: Wellesley, Smith, Vassar and Radcliffe. With the exception of Penn and Columbia, located in cities with large Jewish populations, most of the alma maters of my classmates had a history of exclusionary policies when it came to Jews—both in admitting students and hiring faculty— with official quotas having been only recently rescinded and unofficial practices and personally held prejudices still likely present. All of which exacerbated my growing discomfort as I began to fidget with my tie, finally loosening it so I could breathe more easily.

And then there was the matter of the names. There were several juniors and a number of II's and some III's, like E. Ellsworth McMeen III, and even a Charles Dar-

The Tree of Sorrow

ling IV. I estimated about 20% of the students' surnames were likely Jewish which made me feel like I was back at Thomas Williams Junior High with some Jews but not enough to prevent being required to rise for the Lord's Prayer.

The fact that I was uncomfortable with the milieu at Penn, particularly during the first year, was not just due to the demographics of the school nor any possible latent anti-Semitism but rather because of what was inside me. My roots remained firmly embedded in the soil of Strawberry Mansion and Gilbert Street where I grew up from the time of my birth until my bar mitzvah. I felt accustomed to being among Jews, and most important of all, I felt safe. The outside world, the world of the Gentiles, caused me pause if not downright fear—the fear of being forced from my bike and beaten to the fear of being carted from my home, corralled into a cattle car, and taken to some remote place to be shot, gassed or worked to death. No matter whether the fear was well founded or not, it was there, inside of me. Like a tree, my roots held me in place and if uprooted, I would not survive. But also, like a tree, my trunk could grow; branches could sprout and expand; leaves could bud so long as I remained ensconced in the soil from which I sprang.

By the middle of the first week of law school, I shed the suit for a sport jacket and open-collar shirt. By the next week, the sport jacket was gone. I wore jeans and loafers and pullovers and shirts. After a few weeks, my briefcase remained home, and I carried my books instead. I didn't feel like I did in Mt. Airy or at Temple and certainly not like I had in AZA, but I was growing acclimated to my new surroundings, and after I passed all my mid-terms, I was no longer as intimidated by the caliber of my fellow students. I made a few friends during my matriculation, nothing close or lasting, but it was not my purpose to do so. I was there for something else.

Something deep inside me inspired me to become a lawyer. In college, there were times I had considered other paths: social work, teaching on the college level, becoming a writer. And indeed, I would be a writer and do some teaching as well. But what motivated me then was so powerful and overwhelming, it could not be denied. I had to be a lawyer because of what Oma said.

Every so often, I am inexplicably drawn to the framed picture in my study taken in Fairmount Park when I was about three and standing between Oma and Opa. It's almost as if I am being beckoned. In the past when gazing at the photo, I always saw Oma staring down at me with apprehension. But maybe there was something more than concern in her expression that I had not seen before. Now when I look and see her face, I see the same look that accompanied the one word Oma spoke each time I'd tell her that I was planning to go to law school. "*Gerechtigkeit*," she would say. "Justice," I would think.

It now seems that after all these years I had been missing something. Oma was not just opining that *gerechtigkeit* was part of my nature and that becoming a lawyer was a wise vocational choice for me. Yes, that was part of it. But the most important thing she meant didn't register with me at the time. Which should come as no surprise because our ability to converse deeply and subtly was very much hampered by the fact she spoke German and I spoke English. The concoction of English and German in which we communicated when I was young worked well at the time but was ill suited for adult conversation. So, I was oblivious to what Oma was trying to tell me so many times that final year of her life.

The Tree of Sorrow

What Oma wanted me to know was that I must always strive for *gerechtigkeit*. Even if I had to fight for it. This was not just a philosophical observation. It was as existential as existential can get. It arose from her own lived life, passed down to me in the biblical command, "Justice, Justice You Shall Pursue." Demand Justice. Battle Injustice. And what more of an injustice than the Holocaust? Never allow it or anything like it to happen again. Insist on it as a lawyer. Live it like a human being every day of your life. Remember. Never forget.

I grew up a sapling in a forest filled with barren trees: twisted trunks and bent branches, peeling bark and leafless stems, yet not lifeless. The branches whipped in the wind, and the trunks withstood the gusts of time, and the bark bristled against the storms. There were no leaves to cast a shadow, and yet, a shadow darkened the entire forest nonetheless. I have always lived under that shadow even after I left the forest far behind me. It was never an impediment but informed who I am and what I do including the pursuit of justice whenever injustice rears its head. What other way to remember the Holocaust and honor its victims?

Epilogue

The next seven years of my life were busy indeed. I graduated from law school, served as an assistant district attorney but only for a year and a half which is all the time it took me to know that I was not cut out to be a prosecutor, joined with three other young lawyers to start a law firm, founded a mortgage banking company, and moved with Frani into a house Dad had built to encourage us to have his grandchildren, which we accomplished with the births of our two sons.

With the exception of my time in law school, I have been writing since the age of twelve. I like to say this hiatus was because studying the law has a way of sucking the creative juices out of a person. In any event, with law school behind me, I resumed writing as much as time allowed which often wasn't much more than a half hour or so late at night.

My first published piece was a poem that appeared in a small literary journal in 1977. Though I have no idea why, I never wrote or published a poem again. My second publication was a work of nonfiction, published

The Tree of Sorrow

a year later, that appeared in the Philadelphia Jewish Exponent in a section of selected essays and literary pieces. It appears below and speaks for itself.

The Tree of Sorrow

In 1957 he died, so this day happened sometime before then. Maybe I was eight or nine; it does not matter.

He stood tall, and loomed above me wearing his gray vested suit, big brown shoes and his gray hat with the brim turned slightly down. He was smoking his worn pipe, which was partially bitten through, and he gazed down at me with smiling and sparkling blue eyes.

They speak of him as though his impressive stature was something of the past—before the concentration camp from which he was carried out on a stretcher. They say he never regained his former countenance. Yet to me, he was massive and powerful. And I called him "Opa."

A chain ran from his vest pocket to the baggy pocket in his pants. Attached to the chain was a tarnished silver watch. Often during the course of the day, he would retrieve his watch from its lodging so that it might inform him of the time. His life, while no longer busy and complicated was nevertheless orderly and punctual. There was a definite time of the day to eat or to take a walk or to read "Aufbau," a German-Jewish newspaper. But on this particular day, he brought forth the watch to show his oldest grandson.

"On your Bar Mitzvah, Richard, I will give you this watch." The words were spoken in German, but I understood them. He held the watch up for me to see, and then slowly and deliberately returned it to his vest pocket.

Richard D. Bank

He died three years before my Bar Mitzvah, but I never forgot that day—the watch—the words spoken to me—the smile in his eyes when he looked at me.

When I was married, I took the watch with me. I left many things of my childhood behind in my parents' home, but the watch was not one of them; it went with me.

I kept the watch and its chain in a box with a rubber band around it so the watch would not fall out. The box stayed in a drawer. But the watch had an unusual past—it had its own special story.

As best as I can discern, the watch was given to my grandfather on his Bar Mitzvah. I do not know if it was new then, and I cannot assume such was the case, since his family placed great value on tradition and the past. Even now, without the aid of a genealogist, I can trace his family to 1776.

Naturally, my grandfather kept this watch. As he grew older and prosperous, he acquired other watches, including one very valuable gold pocket watch.

But despite acceptance, success, respectability and even German-born ancestors going back for generations, he was a Jew and nothing but a Jew when Hitler assumed control of Germany. He and my grandmother were sent to a concentration camp—Theresienstadt, where they remained until the end of the war.

His gold watch was taken from him, along with everything else of value to the Third Reich. However, he was permitted to keep the old and tarnished silver watch from his Bar Mitzvah, and the watch stayed with him in the camp.

I do not know the "why," but my grandparents both survived the Holocaust. Physically, psychologically and emotionally battered and torn, my grandparents emerged from Theresienstadt alive. My grandmother bore her yellow Star of David and other badges of distinction. My

The Tree of Sorrow

grandfather came out with his tarnished silver pocket watch; the watch that marked time witnessing the horrors of the Holocaust. The watch was also a survivor, and it was destined for me.

When I was approaching my 30th birthday, I was giving careful thought to the special gift of my choosing which my wife had offered to buy me. My attention turned to my grandfather's watch, kept almost clandestinely in a drawer for many years.

I opened the box and looked at the watch, as I had from time to time. I tried to start the watch by carefully turning the tiny knob on its top. The watch remained silent.

Nevertheless, I felt even more strongly attracted to it, and I decided I wanted something done with the watch to mark my 30th birthday. The next morning, I put the box containing the watch in the glove compartment of my car, where it remained for several days until I visited my jeweler.

My jeweler is no ordinary jeweler; I consider him an artist. I told him the story of the watch. I told him of my grandfather, the Holocaust, Theresienstadt; my grandfather's promise to me, my feelings about the horrors, the suffering and the deaths, of the survivors, the witnesses, and the confirmation of life. And my jeweler told me of the time when he, as a soldier, helped to liberate some of the concentration camps at the war's end—how he cannot forget what happened, how so many others have forgotten so well.

He began to describe a tree which would be made of silver. The tree would have no branches nor leaves, but instead there would be teardrops coming down its side. The tree would bend at the top, hunched forward with its burden, and there the watch would hang.

He told me that my grandfather's name—Ludwig Frank—would emanate from the tree and sprawl out at the base, returning to the tree at the other side. He spoke softly, saying that this would represent the continuity of life. This would be no ordinary tree, he said, adding, "It shall be the 'Tree of Sorrow.'"

My 30th birthday was made even more special by falling on a Friday. Friday night—the eve of Shabbat—has always been notable for me. I remember as a little boy watching my grandparents welcome Shabbat by lighting the candles and blessing the wine and the bread.

Long ago, I was told of my other grandfather, whose name is my middle name, and his rigid rule of always being home for Friday nights. He would spend those evenings reading—often the Bible, despite the fact he was an agnostic and never attended synagogue.

The tradition was carried on by my own parents, and I felt not an obligation nor a duty, but an overwhelming desire, to do the same. On this particular evening, the Shabbat candles shone brighter than usual. And on this night, I received my gift.

It was as promised. I gently lifted the silver tree out of its box. It was not a bright or shiny silver but darkened and varied in shade. The tree had no branches, and it bent forward at the top. Instead of leaves there were tears, and my grandfather's name was sprawled at the base, which was made of the same silver. The letter "L" emanated from the tree and the last letter returned to the trunk at the other side.

I plucked the watch from the tree and turned its tiny knob. The arms stood still...the second hand did not whirl...the watch remained silent. I returned the watch to the tree, carried it to my den and placed it upon my desk. The watch was at rest.

I have no explanation for what followed. All I can do is relate what happened, and that seems to be enough.

It was the Sunday after my birthday—sometime in the

The Tree of Sorrow

evening. I was looking at my gift. I reached out for it, and, while not meaning to, brushed the watch with my fingers so that the watch rubbed against the tree. The second hand spun around the small dial at the bottom of the watch's face. The watch ticked boldly, and, as I sat transfixed, the minute hand lurched forward. Doubting my senses, I called to my wife. She confirmed what I was seeing.

The next morning the watch stopped, and, despite repeated efforts, it remained mute. That is, until two weeks later, when my mother was visiting and touched her father's watch hanging from the tree. The watch started again. Once more, the instrument offered its message. The next morning it stopped and remained silent.

The jeweler's words echoed through my mind. Out of the ashes of the dead, from the horrors of the Holocaust, there is the continuity of life. And one thing more, I thought. The watch and the tree on which it sits, are more than the remembrance of one man. They also serve as a symbol of the link from one generation to the next, and of the unity of all humanity.

As I write these last lines to this memoir, only a few months remain until my grandson, Hayden Louis Bank, will become a bar mitzvah. Several years ago, as my grandfather had pledged to me when I was younger, I made a promise to Hayden that the watch will be his when he reaches this milestone. There are no conditions or restrictions or requirements regarding this bestowal. It is unqualified and final and absolute. But this time when the watch transitions from grandfather to grandson, it will not be alone. It will be linked with hope. Hope that Hayden and his sister, Rebecca, and their generation will convert The Tree of Sorrow to The Tree of Life.

Acknowledgements

For some books to be written, certain prerequisites must be met. This has never been the case with any of my books until now and thus I am grateful to three people who have made this memoir possible. First, if it were not for the German historian, Roland Paul, who several years ago reached out to my family and provided information about the Frank's, I would never have known that my grandfather had two brothers, a sister, and nieces and nephews murdered in the Holocaust. Silence runs deep and only because of Roland have I come to realize how deep. The next individual, the second generation of a four generation family of jewelers, is Mitchell Rosnov and without him, there literally would be no "Tree of Sorrow." This is explained in the Epilogue.

The third person who made this book possible is my wife, Frani, who had she chosen, could have thwarted this project but chose not to. One reason our marriage had passed the golden anniversary milestone is because Frani never sees any of my work until publication, including this book. But a memoir is by its nature very personal, and I can only imagine her apprehension over what I might write about or reveal. But with the exception of a restrained twist of the lips whenever someone asked what I was currently working on, Frani maintained her silence and composure thus allowing me unbridled freedom to write *The Tree of Sorrow.*

With the writing complete, there was no question in my mind where to take it. The first pair of eyes to see the manuscript was the publisher of my last book,

Dr. Shrikrishna Singh, the owner of Auctus Publishers. Krish and I have become very good friends and we share the belief that one should pursue one's passion. Thus, Krish has two requirements of his authors: that they exhibit quality writing and are passionate about their work. I couldn't have found a better home for my books than Auctus.

When the time arrived for editing, I asked Krish if Alexa Flood who edited my last book would be available and was thrilled to learn she would edit my current manuscript. With Alexa's keen eye, perceptive insight, and resolute fact checking, I was able to concentrate on the writing knowing Alexa was looking over my shoulder. I did not know Colleen Cummings who would be responsible for the typesetting and design of the book and cover but I knew *The Tree of Sorrow* was in exceptional hands when she indicated at the start how she would delve into the text to make certain the cover art and interior book design would reflect the tone of the story. In this regard, Colleen succeeded beyond expectations so that the book's motif remains with the reader from beginning to end.

The final member of the team is my grandson, Hayden Louis Bank, who became a bar mitzvah this year. As he did for my last book, Hayden provided the photography for the cover and this time he supplied the photos for the chapter illustrations as well. Hayden is also to be credited with the family tree appearing in this book which is only a fragment of the extensive project he is completing for the Frank family spanning eight generations. Even more, Hayden's fervor to learn about his family and his people, and to contribute to this rumination of the past, fills me with hope for a better future.

www.ingramcontent.com/pod-product-compliance
Lightning Source LLC
Chambersburg PA
CBHW071848070526
44583CB00016B/1593